A TIME
TO BUILD

CREATING SEXUALLY HEALTHY
FAITH COMMUNITIES

Second Edition

by Rev. Debra W. Haffner

Religious Institute

ISBN 978-0-9855949-0-9

Religious Declaration on Sexual Morality, Justice, and Healing

Sexuality is God's life-giving and life-fulfilling gift. We come from diverse religious communities to recognize sexuality as central to our humanity and as integral to our spirituality. We are speaking out against the pain, brokenness, oppression and loss of meaning that many experience about their sexuality.

Our faith traditions celebrate the goodness of creation, including our bodies and our sexuality. We sin when this sacred gift is abused or exploited. However, the great promise of our traditions is love, healing and restored relationships.

Our culture needs a sexual ethic focused on personal relationships and social justice rather than particular sexual acts. All persons have the right and responsibility to lead sexual lives that express love, justice, mutuality, commitment, consent and pleasure. Grounded in respect for the body and for the vulnerability that intimacy brings, this ethic fosters physical, emotional and spiritual health. It accepts no double standards and applies to all persons, without regard to sex, gender, color, age, bodily condition, marital status or sexual orientation.

God hears the cries of those who suffer from the failure of religious communities to address sexuality. We are called today to see, hear and respond to the suffering caused by sexual abuse and violence against women and lesbian, gay, bisexual and transgender (LGBT) persons, the HIV pandemic, unsustainable population growth and over-consumption, and the commercial exploitation of sexuality.

Faith communities must therefore be truth-seeking, courageous and just. We call for:
- Theological reflection that integrates the wisdom of excluded, often silenced peoples, and insights about sexuality from medicine, social science, the arts and humanities.
- Full inclusion of women and LGBT persons in congregational life, including their ordination and marriage equality.
- Sexuality counseling and education throughout the lifespan from trained religious leaders.
- Support for those who challenge sexual oppression and who work for justice within their congregations and denominations.

Faith communities must also advocate for sexual and spiritual wholeness in society. We call for:
- Lifelong, age-appropriate sexuality education in schools, seminaries and community settings.
- A faith-based commitment to sexual and reproductive rights, including access to voluntary contraception, abortion, and HIV/STD prevention and treatment.
- Religious leadership in movements to end sexual and social injustice.

God rejoices when we celebrate our sexuality with holiness and integrity. We, the undersigned, invite our colleagues and faith communities to join us in promoting sexual morality, justice, and healing.

Updated January 2010

© 2012 Religious Institute, Inc.
ISBN 978-0-9855949-0-9

TABLE OF
CONTENTS

ACKNOWLEDGEMENTS 4

INTRODUCTION 5

    RELIGION AND SEXUALITY 6

    HOW TO USE THIS GUIDEBOOK 11

THE BUILDING BLOCKS 13

    SEXUALLY HEALTHY RELIGIOUS PROFESSIONALS 13

    WORSHIP AND PREACHING 17

    PASTORAL CARE 24

    EDUCATION FOR YOUTH 30

    ADULT EDUCATION 44

    WELCOMING AND AFFIRMING CONGREGATIONS 49

    SAFE CONGREGATIONS 56

    SOCIAL ACTION 62

RESOURCES FOR MORE INFORMATION 70

REFERENCES 74

ACKNOWLEDGEMENTS

Many people provided guidance and input on the development of this guide.

The first edition of A *Time to Build: Creating Sexually Healthy Faith Communities* was published in 2002 as the first publication of the then newly formed Religious Institute. Its publication was funded by the W.T. Grant Foundation, one of the first foundations to support the Religious Institute.

The first edition was written as my master's thesis at Union Theological Seminary with the encouragement of my faculty advisors Rev. Barbara Lundblad and Professor Kathy Talvacchia. In the ten years since, I have had the privilege of working with hundreds of congregations, thousands of clergy and seminarians, and lay leaders from more than twenty-five denominations in every state in the country. I have also had the opportunity to work with denomination leaders and the leaders of organizations that advocate sexual health and rights in faith communities. I've also had the good fortune to work as the endorsed community minister at the Unitarian Church in Westport for the past decade.

I have learned a great deal about congregational life and leadership in these intervening ten years, and the landscape of how congregations are engaging sexuality issues has expanded considerably. Thus, it was time to develop this completely updated edition of A *Time to Build*.

I am grateful to Amanda Winters for updating the statistics and resources for this new edition and to Blanca Godoi for her research and careful preparation of the manuscript through its many drafts and revisions. I am indebted to Marie Alford-Harkey, Michael Cobb, the Rev. Carla Dietz, the Rev. Cedric Harmon, the Rev. Carolyn Patierno, and the Rev. Alida Ward for their careful review and suggestions. I am so appreciative of the magical editing of Holly Sprunger and the design work of Alan Barnett.

This update is dedicated to the co-founder of the Religious Institute, the Reverend Dr. Larry Greenfield. Without his support and encouragement, the Religious Institute would not have come into being in 2001. He was an early mentor as I began my path to ministry and encouraged and supported me as the first edition was created. I am pleased that he continues as a the Chair of the Board of Directors of the Religious Institute, as my colleague, and as my friend.

— *Rev. Debra W. Haffner*

INTRODUCTION

Sexuality is God's life-giving and life-fulfilling gift. We come from diverse religious communities to recognize sexuality as central to our humanity and as integral to our spirituality. We are speaking out against the pain, brokenness, oppression, and loss of meaning that many experience about their sexuality.

———————— ☯ ————————

*T*he **Religious Declaration on Sexual Morality, Justice, and Healing,** first published in 2000 and updated in 2010, is a clarion call to the nation's religious denominations, congregations, and clergy. It calls for a sexual ethic focused on personal relationships and social justice rather than particular sexual acts.

The **Religious Declaration** is a positive vision of the relationship between sexuality and spirituality, grounded in the core teachings of the historic faiths. It urges religious leaders and faith communities to provide comprehensive sexuality education and to advocate for sexual and reproductive rights, and full inclusion of women and lesbian, gay, bisexual and transgender persons (LGBT) in congregational life, seminaries, denominations, and society at large.

More than 3,600 clergy and theologians from more than 70 faith traditions have endorsed the **Religious Declaration.**

The **Religious Declaration** challenges congregations to be sexually healthy faith communities. A sexually healthy faith community promotes the integration of sexuality and spirituality in worship, preaching, pastoral care, youth and adult religious education, and social action programs in the community. It makes a commitment to a sexual ethic that is not based on double standards and understands that dealing with sexuality is an issue of spiritual wholeness. A congregation that addresses sexuality openly and holistically models that sexuality and spirituality are intimately connected.

A **Time to Build** was developed to help clergy and congregations create sexually healthy faith communities.

A sexually healthy faith community is committed to fostering spiritual, sexual, and emotional health among the congregation and providing a safe environment where sexuality issues are addressed with respect, mutuality, and openness. The eight building blocks are:

- Sexually healthy religious professionals with training and experience in sexuality issues.
- Worship and preaching periodically on sexuality issues.
- Sexuality education for children and youth.
- Sexuality education and support for adults.
- Welcome and full inclusion for LGBT individuals and families.
- A commitment to being a Safe Congregation, against sexual exploitation of all kinds, including sexual abuse, sexual harassment, and sexual misconduct by staff and clergy.
- Social action efforts for sexual justice in society.

RELIGION AND SEXUALITY

Our faith traditions celebrate the goodness of creation, including our bodies and our sexuality. We sin when this sacred gift is abused or exploited. However, the great promise of our traditions is love, healing, and restored relationships.

———————— ☯ ————————

Our religious traditions affirm that sexuality is a divinely bestowed blessing for the purposes of expressing love, generating new life, and providing companionship and pleasure. They recognize the unique role that a faith community can play in helping adults live in a manner that reflects the holiness within each person and within relationships. They celebrate the goodness of creation, including our bodies and our sexuality. They affirm that we are co-creators of a world that affirms justice, love, and rightful relations. They are committed to "understanding sexual pleasure as a moral good rooted in the sacred value of our sensuality and erotic power."[1] They teach that it is in our relationships with others that we understand God's love for us, and it is in our experience of our sexuality that we come closest to being revealed to others.

The theological foundation for the *Religious Declaration* draws on a broad range of sources: scripture, religious tradition, denominational policies, human experience, science, and reason. The creators of the *Religious Declaration* were not trying to develop a new sexual theology, but rather to articulate an extant theology about sexuality that is grounded in religious tradition and thinking. The box on pages 8 to 9 includes sections of reports on sexuality from many denominations. (The Reading List on page 46 contains important books on the theology of sexuality. The questions in the study guidebook on page 48 will help readers explore these theological concerns.)

Every faith community in America—whether progressive or conservative, liberal or evangelical—is called to address the sexuality needs of their congregants. All clergy counsel congregants who struggle with sexual issues. Almost every faith community understands that the sacred gift of sexuality can be abused or exploited: they have witnessed domestic violence, adolescent pregnancy, sexual abuse, sexual harassment, homophobia, sexism, and sexual exploitation. Almost all have recognized the importance of sexuality education for their teenagers; some have made a commitment to lifelong sexuality education. Denominations in America have struggled with issues related to sexual orientation and gender identity with some now voting to ordain gay, lesbian, bisexual, and transgendered clergy and to perform same-sex marriages. Too many denominations have been roiled by cases of sexual misconduct by clergy. The reality is, in the words of Reverend Cynthia Breen, that "sexuality is simply too important, too beautiful, and too potentially dangerous to be ignored in a religious community."[2]

Religion is central to the lives of most adults in America. More than eight in ten American adults say that religion is important in their lives and more than six in ten say that it is very important to them. More than four in ten Americans attend a worship service weekly and six in ten do so monthly. One-third of adults participate in religious education programs, and one-third do community volunteer work through their congregation.[3]

Sex and sexuality are no less central to Americans. We are surrounded by sexual messages in the television we watch, the movies we attend, the news we read, the music we hear, and the constant use of sexual images in advertisements. The vast majority of American adults, whether single or married, young or old, gay, straight, or bisexual, are sexually involved: only 10 percent of adult men and only 13 percent of adult women did not have partnered sex in the past year.[4]

Moreover, people want their religious institution to help them with sexuality issues. For example, in a study conducted by the United Church of Christ, more than eight out of ten members said they looked to their church as a resource on sexuality-related decisions and concerns.[5]

DEFINITIONS OF SEXUAL HEALTH

"Sexual health is a state of physical, emotional, mental, and social wellbeing in relation to sexuality; it is not merely the absence of disease, dysfunction, or infirmity. Sexual health needs a positive and respectful approach to sexuality and sexual relationships, and the possibility of having pleasurable and safe sexual experiences that are free of coercion, discrimination, and violence. For sexual health to be attained and maintained, the sexual rights of all individuals must be respected, protected, and satisfied."

—World Health Organization, 2006

"We must understand that sexuality encompasses more than sexual behavior, that the many aspects of sexuality include not only the physical, but the mental and spiritual as well, and that sexuality is a core component of personality… Sexual health is not limited to the absence of disease or dysfunction, nor is its importance confined to just the reproductive years. It includes the ability to understand and weigh the risks, responsibilities, outcomes, and impacts of sexual action and to practice abstinence when appropriate. It includes freedom from sexual abuse and discrimination and the ability of individuals to integrate their sexuality into their lives, derive pleasure from it, and to reproduce if they so choose."

—Surgeon General of the United States, 2001[4]

DENOMINATION STATEMENTS ON SEXUALITY ISSUES

Many denominations have adopted formal theological statements about sexuality. Below are statements from a range of Jewish and Christian religious denominations; because no such centralized body exists for Muslim or Eastern traditions, they are not included, although there are sacred texts in these religions that affirm the goodness of sexuality. Despite denomination differences, they are remarkably similar in their understanding of the goodness of creation, our bodies, and our sexuality as well as the potential for misuse and abuse. The reader is encouraged to read the statements to gain insights into the broad theological support that affirms sexuality as a central, sacred part of human life as well as to understand the position of one's own tradition. The Religious Institute maintains an online clearinghouse of denomination statements on a wide range of sexuality issues. To find out what a particular denomination says, go to religiousinstitute.org/denominational-statements.

Catechism of the
Catholic Church
"Sexuality affects all aspects of the human person in the unity of his body and soul. It especially concerns affectivity, the capacity to love and to procreate, and in a more general way the aptitude for forming bonds of communion with others."[5]

Church of the Brethren, 1983
"Sexuality is elemental in human beings...This sexuality enriches human relationships in ways that are basic to God's own nature (Gen. 1:27). Furthermore, it offers human beings partnership with God in holy creation and re-creation (Gen. 1:28). In their enjoyment of these privileges concomitant with sexuality, God's people are to be responsible. The church identifies love and covenant as two guidelines for sexual responsibility."[6]

Episcopal Church, 2003
"Sexuality is a fundamental and complex aspect of human nature...As Christians we believe it is part of God's good creation and intended to be a source of blessing and joy for human beings...The links between love and sexual pleasure testify to the way in which sexuality blesses human intimacy. Sexual intimacy has a public and social dimension as well. When healthy and well-ordered, our sexuality and sexual expressions contribute to the health and stability of individuals and society."[7]

Evangelical Lutheran
Church in America, 2009
"God created human beings to be in relationship with each other and continually blesses us with diverse powers, which we use in living out those relationships ... Sexuality especially involves the powers or capacities to form deep and lasting bonds, to give and receive pleasure, and to conceive and bear children. Sexuality can be integral to the desire to commit oneself to life with another, to touch and be touched, and to love and be loved. Such powers are complex and ambiguous. They can be used well or badly. They can bring astonishing joy and delight. Such powers can serve God and serve the neighbor. They also can hurt self or hurt the neighbor. Sexuality finds expression at the extreme ends of human experience: in love, care, and security, or lust, cold indifference, and exploitation."[8]

Jewish Reconstructionist
Federation, 1993
"Jewish tradition speaks of sexuality as *simchat ona*: the joy of sex, and *simchat ishto*: rejoicing in one's partner...In Judaism, physical pleasure and sexual responsibility are inextricably linked. Jewish tradition has always regarded sexuality as a powerful force that needs self-regulation. The expression of sexuality must take place in light of the values and norms that shapes its proper place in human life."[9]

Metropolitan Community Churches, 2007
"We believe that our sexuality is a holy gift from God so we no longer distance our bodies from our experience with God. We are a people who proudly participate in the communion of body and spirit."[10]

Reform Judaism, Central Conference of American Rabbis, 1998
"Sexuality and sexual expression are integral and powerful elements in the potential wholeness of human beings. Our tradition commands us to sanctify the basic elements of the human being through values that express the Divine in every person and in every relationship. Each Jew should seek to conduct his/her sexual life in a manner that elicits the intrinsic holiness within the person and the relationship."[11]

Unitarian Universalist Association, 2011
"We believe that God, or the sacred, permeates all aspects of life on this earth, and that sexuality is a very strong force in human life. We can't know God as separate, pure, ethereal—we only know God as interwoven into our beings, our relationships, our total lives, imperfect as these may be! Human sexuality is an aspect of life which can allow us to experience God's love for our bodies and our souls. The sacred is known in radical mutuality, interdependence, the sheer knowing that our own joy and fulfillment are inseparable from that of others."[12]

The United Methodist Church, 2008
"We affirm that sexuality is God's good gift to all persons. We call everyone to responsible stewardship of this sacred gift…All persons, regardless of age, gender, marital status, or sexual orientation, are entitled to have their human and civil rights ensured and to be protected against violence. The Church should support the family in providing age-appropriate education regarding sexuality to children, youth, and adults.

We affirm that all persons are individuals of sacred worth, created in the image of God. All persons need the ministry of the Church in their struggles for human fulfillment, as well as the spiritual and emotional care of a fellowship that enables reconciling relationships with God, with others, and with self."[13]

United Church of Christ, 1997
"All that we are, including our sexuality, is a gift of God…We as sexual creatures are created free to use the gifts of life and of sexuality in ways that ennoble and endear—or betray and demean. The freedom is a gift to have, to hold, to express, to share. We as sexual creatures are made for relationship, for community. The church is that special form of community through which we experience the fullness of grace, God's presence in trial and rejoicing, and the promise of hope, power, and love in its forms of agape, philia, and eros. Stewards of the gift of sexuality: that is who we are. Pray God for faithful stewardship!"[14]

HEALING THE SUFFERING

Sexual diseases and sexual disease plague America. Too many Americans experience suffering related to sexuality rather than experiencing it as a life-fulfilling gift. These are national statistics, but they are likely mirrored in most communities.

Almost half of all pregnancies in the United States are unintended.[15]

Approximately 750,000 teenage women become pregnant each year. The United States' teen pregnancy rate is almost three times that of Germany and France, and over four times that of the Netherlands, despite that the age of sexual debut is similar in these countries.[16]

The U.S. Centers for Disease Control and Prevention estimates that there are approximately 19 million new sexually transmitted infections (STI) each year — almost half of them among young people 15 to 24 years of age.[17]

Sixty-five million Americans have at least one viral STI, most commonly genital herpes.[18]

The U.S. Centers for Disease Control and Prevention estimates that undiagnosed and untreated STDs cause at least 24,000 women in the United States each year to become infertile.[19]

Since the AIDS epidemic began, more than 576,000 people with AIDS in the United States have died; more than 18,000 people with AIDS still die each year.[20]

More than one million people are living with HIV infection in the United States.[21]

One in five people living with HIV is unaware of their infection.[22]

God hears the cries of those who suffer from the failure of religious communities to address sexuality. We are called today to see, hear and respond to the suffering caused by sexual abuse and violence against women and lesbian, gay, bisexual and transgender (LGBT) persons, the HIV pandemic, unsustainable population growth and over-consumption, and the commercial exploitation of sexuality.

Nearly 9 in 10 (85%) LGBT teens report being verbally harassed; 40% report being physically harassed; and 19% reported being physically assaulted at school because of their sexual orientation.[23]

Of the estimated 1.6 million homeless American youth, between 20 and 40 percent identify as lesbian, gay, bisexual or transgender (LGBT).[24]

In an Indiana University study, the rate of condom use for penile-vaginal sex was 80% for teen (14–17) males and 69% for females.[25] But condom use declined with age and by the time people reach 50, only one in five men and one in four women used a condom at last intercourse.

An estimated 135,000 children are sexually abused each year in the United States.[26]

One in four women and one in six men experience child sexual abuse before age 18.[27]

Every two minutes, someone in the United States is sexually assaulted.[28]

One out of every six American women has been the victim of an attempted or completed rape in her lifetime. About 3% of American men—or 1 in 33—have experienced an attempted or completed rape in their lifetime.[29]

An estimated 1.3 million women are victims of physical assault by an intimate partner each year.[30]

HOW TO USE THIS GUIDEBOOK

4.5 aortic onveriom 6 mos. check

*T*his guidebook describes the eight building blocks for a sexually healthy faith community. It includes sections on sexually healthy religious professionals, policies and environment, pastoral care, worship and preaching, safe congregations, youth and adult education, welcoming and affirming congregations, and social action. It offers ideas and suggestions that congregations can adapt for their own theology and traditions.

Becoming a sexually healthy faith community is a process. A congregation may not feel it is ready to hold an after-school comprehensive sexuality education program for teens. It may, however, feel ready for an evening program for parents on handling sexuality issues in their homes in the context of the faith tradition. Some individuals may experience surprise to hear the minister or the rabbi address a sexuality issue from the pulpit; preaching about creation and embodiment is often a good starting point.

There are a number of ways that a congregation leader or clergyperson can use this guidebook. Ministers, rabbis, and imams for example, do not need permission to offer pastoral counseling on a sexuality issue or to preach about a sexuality topic. Other areas, such as implementing a sexuality education program or developing policies addressing sexual harassment, will probably need the support of the important lay committees, such as the leadership, social justice/outreach committee, religious education committee or youth committee. Many congregations experience tension around such sexuality issues as abortion or LGBT full inclusion, and may want to begin work, for example, on safe congregations policies or sexuality education for parents before tackling more controversial areas. Not all of the suggestions will make sense for every faith community, and some may seem more appropriate for larger congregations or ones with more experience addressing sexuality issues. Look at what's useful; discard what is not. Feel free to adapt any of the material in this guidebook.

Throughout the guidebook, at the end of each building block, the reader will find a checklist of assessment questions to assess the congregation's current policies and programs as well as resource boxes for more information. Each checklist includes a "Plan for Improvement" box to jot down ideas for new or improved efforts or to mark "not applicable" or "not now." Few congregations will check "yes" for every suggestion; they are presented here as ideas for your consideration. The Resource List that is included with each building block is a list of organizations for more information.

There are a variety of ways to use the checklists. The clergy, religious educator, or lay leader may want to begin by reading the guidebook and thinking through which areas can be addressed first. Some congregations have developed a steering committee on sexuality issues to conduct an overall assessment and develop a plan to improve the sexual health of the congregation. A group of lay and professional staff could receive training in sexuality to become

"Sexuality Resource Persons" or the "Sexuality Task Force." This could be a new committee with the goal of fostering sexual health in the congregation or to begin by completing the assessments in this guidebook. It could also have a specific function such as to offer programs on religion and sexuality within the congregation or survey congregation members on their interest and commitment to becoming a sexually healthy faith community. It could also lead a worship service or an adult education program. Other congregations may want to divide the guidebook into sections based on their committee structure: e.g., the religious educator might take the sexuality education section; the lay leadership might take the section on policies and procedures.

Once the assessments are completed by the whole committee or the subgroups, leaders will want to meet together to discuss the congregation's existing strengths addressing sexuality issues, areas that could be improved and addressed, which areas are not going to be pursued at this time, and ideas for plans for improvement. An annual plan including any budget implications can be developed by the lay and ministerial leadership for a one, two, or three-year period.

Ultimately, a commitment to developing a sexually health faith community needs to be shared by every part of the community. The clergy, religious educators, the lay leadership, key committee members, the parents, the youth, indeed every member of the community, must share the commitment to sexual and spiritual wholeness. Sexual health is not limited to the adult or youth education program or the clergy's willingness and ability to discuss sexuality issues. These are important, but not enough. We are called in community to promote sexual morality, justice, and healing. This guidebook is offered to assist congregations in that process.

SEXUALLY HEALTHY RELIGIOUS PROFESSIONALS

One of the most important building blocks for a sexually healthy congregation is a staff of sexually healthy religious professionals. Sexually healthy religious professionals—clergy, religious educators, and pastoral counselors—are comfortable with their own sexuality, have the skills to provide pastoral care and worship on sexuality issues, and are committed to sexual justice in the congregation and the society at large. The self-assessment on pages 15 to 16 identifies many of the characteristics and qualities of a sexually healthy religious professional.

In brief, sexually healthy religious professionals are:

- Knowledgeable about human sexuality;
- Familiar with their tradition's sacred text on sexuality;
- Able to engage in theological reflection about how best to integrate sexuality and spirituality;
- Able to examine the impact of racism, sexism, heterosexism and homophobia in ministry;
- Trained in pastoral counseling approaches that facilitate resolution of interpersonal conflict, specifically when dealing with sexual matters, for individuals, families and groups;
- Able to serve as role models, discussing sexual issues with ease and comfort;
- Knowledgeable about their denomination's policies on sexuality;
- Able to speak out for sexual justice within their denomination and in the larger community;
- Skillful in preaching about sexuality-related issues;
- Able to recognize their own personal limitations and boundaries when it comes to handling sexuality issues;
- Able to deal appropriately with sexual feelings that may arise for congregants, and vice-versa.

Ideally, clergy and religious educators would have formal graduate-level training in human sexuality. According to the Pan American Health Organization, professions that address sexuality issues should have "basic knowledge of human sexuality, awareness of personal attitudes towards one's own and other people's sexuality which should include a respectful attitude towards persons with different sexual orientations and sexual practices, and basic skills in identifying, and if necessary, referring to the appropriate professional, problems of sexual health."[31]

Unfortunately, only a small number of seminaries prepare their clergy to handle sexuality issues, and many clergy provide sexuality counseling without the benefit of formal training. Over the last two decades, a number of studies have reported that seminarians and clergy feel unprepared and ill-equipped to deal with a range of sexuality-related issues. Further, many denominations have been roiled by instances of clergy misconduct.

In 2001, the Seminary Sexuality Education Survey, conducted by Sally Conklin, investigated how seminary training prepared clergy to address the sexuality-related needs of congregants. This 2001 survey evaluated course offerings and course content. The survey concluded that "those preparing for ministry were not helped to understand their own sexual values or behaviors, and where there were courses in sexuality, they were not required or connected to the core curriculum."[32]

In 2004, a survey of graduates of five evangelical seminaries between 1992 and 2002 reported that minimal attention was given to understanding and maintaining sexual health or managing feelings of sexual attraction in professional contexts. Researchers concluded that incidents of abuse are reduced and graduates are clearer on sexual misconduct with the training they had received, but they do not know what to do with feelings of sexual attraction to congregants. [33]

In a 2008 survey of progressive clergy—those who support comprehensive sex education, reproductive justice, LGBT equality—fewer than four in ten (38%) agreed that their seminary education adequately prepared them for dealing with sexuality issues in their congregations. Only one-third (35%) agreed that their seminaries adequately prepared them for dealing with sexual orientation, gender identity and gender expression in their congregations.[34]

In 2009, the Religious Institute conducted an intensive study of 36 seminaries in the United States. The study found that most future clergy can graduate from seminary without taking a single sexuality course.[35] More than 9 in 10 of the seminaries surveyed did not require full-semester sexuality issues for religious professionals or LGBT courses for graduation. Only one seminary required a course in sexuality issues for religious professionals, and only two required an LGBT/ queer studies course. Indeed, the study found that courses focusing on sexuality-related issues were often absent from seminary curricula. Most of the seminaries in the survey did not offer full-semester sexuality-related courses. Two-thirds did not have a course in sexuality issues for religious professionals. Three-quarters did not have an LGBT/queer studies course. Where courses existed, fewer than 1 in 10 of the seminaries offered them every semester or every year.[36]

As a result of the Religious Institute study, several seminaries have begun to improve their program offerings and their institutional environments to become sexually healthy and responsible seminaries. There are now at least twenty seminaries in the U.S. that meet the criteria of a sexually healthy seminary. Further, several denominations now require competency in sexual health for all of their ministerial candidates. (See the list on page 70 for seminaries that meet these criteria.)

Religious leaders are encouraged to use the self-assessment on pages 15 to 16 to identify their strengths and weaknesses and develop a plan to address where they need help.

SELF-ASSESSMENT
Characteristics of Sexually Healthy Religious Professionals

On a scale of "1" to "5" (with "5" being the highest possible score),
rate yourself on these characteristics of a sexually healthy religious professional.
Notice if one area needs strengthening and develop plans to address it.

PERSONAL ATTRIBUTES

Sexually healthy religious professionals:

5 have examined their own personal sexual history.

3 have explored their own sexual attitudes and confronted their own limitations and biases about sexuality.

4 have listened to the attitudes of others about sexuality, which are different from their own.

2 have worked if needed with a trained counselor on issues related to personal sexual history.

5 are knowledgeable about human sexuality, including sexual behaviors, sexual response, sexual and gender orientation, and relationships.

4 undertake theological reflection regarding the integration of sexuality and spirituality.

4 model ease and comfort in discussing sexual issues.

5 interact with people of all genders and ages in respectful and appropriate ways.

5 affirm their own sexual orientation and gender identity and respect the sexual orientation and gender identity of others.

5 recognize and affirm family diversity.

5 have personal relationships that express love and intimacy in ways congruent with their own values about sexuality.

1 have taken a graduate-level course on human sexuality.

1 seek ongoing opportunities for education and information regarding sexuality.

47 Total

Score Range 13 to 65
A lower score in this area indicates the need for structured opportunities to explore personal attitudes and feelings about sexuality in one's own life and in others' lives. It may also be helpful to speak with colleagues, staff, trusted congregants, or advisory committee members about their perception of you in this area. A sexuality course for religious professionals or a graduate-level course in human sexuality could prove helpful.

CONGREGATIONAL SKILLS

Sexually healthy religious professionals:

5 have good individual, family, and couples counseling skills.

5 recognize and respect their own personal limitations and boundaries for handling sexuality issues.

5 are familiar with sacred texts on sexuality and theological affirmations of sexuality and how to share them when appropriate in a counseling setting.

5 know when and where to refer someone who has a sexual issue that they are not prepared to handle.

Continued on page 16

5 use power justly and constructively and recognize the potential for abuse of power.

5 understand that sexual feelings for congregants may arise (and vice versa) and know how to deal with them appropriately, including consulting with a supervisor or colleague.

3 have examined the impact of racism, sexism, heterosexism, and homophobia in ministry.

3 are knowledgeable about educational techniques, including how to present knowledge, help explore attitudes, and develop personal skills.

4 have conflict management and mediation skills.

3 are comfortable and skilled in preaching about sexuality-related issues, including knowledge of sacred texts.

5 identify ethical dilemmas when they arise and seek help when needed.

48 Total

Score Range 12 to 60

A lower score in this area can be addressed by graduate-level courses in education or counseling or through supervision by a more experienced colleague. Every pastoral counselor should have a local referral list of mental health professionals who are recommended as marriage, family, and sex therapists. In addition, each clergy should have either a ministerial relations committee or a clergy network to which they can turn to for help with difficult situations involving power or ethics.

COMMUNITY AND DENOMINATIONAL SKILLS

Sexually healthy religious professionals:

5 are knowledgeable about their denomination's policies on a range of sexuality issues.

5 are knowledgeable about their religion's sacred texts on sexuality.

5 are knowledgeable about church history's teachings on sexuality.

4 are skilled in community advocacy for sexual justice issues.

5 challenge and work to change sex-negative values in the faith community and denomination.

3 speak out regularly for sexual justice and seek opportunities to work in collaboration with others on these issues.

27 Total

Score Range 6 to 30

A lower score in this area indicates the need for research on both denomination and sexuality issues. Throughout this guidebook, there are references to denominational policies and resources that may help. Also see the Religious Institute denominational database at: www.religiousinstitute.org/denominational-statements. Many denominations are struggling with how to deal with sexuality issues; they need your leadership. The section on social action may also provide ideas.

WORSHIP AND PREACHING

*L*ike other issues central to people's lives, clergy can address sexuality from the pulpit. Including sexuality issues in sermons and worship can help congregants understand that sexuality is a sacred gift; that sexuality can be talked about in a respectful and serious manner; that clergy are comfortable talking about sexuality issues (and therefore open to discussing these issues in pastoral counseling); and that there is a prophetic voice on sexual justice.

The *Religious Declaration* suggests numerous topics for worship and preaching. Services could include such themes as sexual justice, HIV/AIDS, sexuality education, sexual abuse and violence, parenting, reproductive health and choice, the changing family, sexual orientation and gender identity. Topics (or sermon titles) suggested by the *Religious Declaration* for sermons might include:

- Sexuality: God's Life-Giving and Life-Fulfilling Gift
- The Goodness of Creation and Our Bodies
- Love: The Foundation for Intimacy
- Sexuality: Religious and Moral?
- Faithfully Celebrating Pleasure in Our Lives
- A Religious Duty: Stopping Violence Against Women and LGBT Persons
- The Religious Challenge of HIV/AIDS
- An End to Sexual Exploitation and Commercialization
- What Does the Bible Really Teach About Families?

- A Religious Responsibility: Sexuality Education in Our Congregation, in Our Schools
- The Faithful Search for Social and Sexual Justice
- Religious Choices about Reproductive Health
- Ancient Wisdom and New Reproductive Technologies
- Celebrating Sexuality with Holiness and Integrity
- Sexual Abuse Prevention
- Honoring Mothers Worldwide on Mother's Day

Samples of sermons on a wide range of sexuality topics can be found at www.religiousinstitute.org/sermons.

Sample Sermons

"Too Important, Too Beautiful, Too Dangerous: A Sermon on Sexuality and Spirituality" Sermon by Rev. Judy Welles

This minister relates the sexuality experiences in her life, and the progress that has been made over the decades, as well as UUA policy history.

"An Ethic of Love" Sermon by Rev. Erica Baron
A minister considers the ethics of working toward sexual health as it relates to education, congregational development and UUA principles.

Sexuality Education

Is Sexuality Education Religious Education? Sermon by Katy Carpman

This sermon discusses why a religious organization is uniquely suited to educating youth about sexuality.

HIV/AIDS

Beyond the Gates of Gilead! Sermon by Zach Mills

This sermon makes use of Jeremiah's response to the destruction of the first temple by the Babylonians to explore the HIV/AIDS pandemic.

Reproductive Justice

Hard Choices Sermon by Reverend Barbara Gerlach

This sermon was written for the anniversary of Roe v. Wade and explores the minister's personal history with abortion.

Surviving, Living, & Thriving: A Hope For All Women Sermon by Sadie Stone

This sermon focuses on Postpartum Depression.

LGBT

Blessed to Be Burdened. Sermon by John-Anthony Burchall

This sermon explores LGBT issues in the Black Church.

LGBT Activism as Ministry Sermon by Rev. Rebecca Voelkel (IWR)

Rev. Voelkel speaks about her own calling to the ministry and her work.

Religious Institute: Speaking Out Against LGBT Bullying

On October 4th 2010 in the Washington Post "On Faith" blog, Rev. Debra Haffner called for all religious leaders to speak out for LGBT youth in response to the recent gay youth suicides. Her call, titled An Open Letter to Religious Leaders on Gay Youth Suicides: It's Time to Act Out Loud, resulted

in sermons across the country. The Religious Institute has gathered some of these sermons on its website.

Your Daughter's a WHAT?! Sermon by Ethel-Marie Underhill

This sermon relates one woman's experience with her daughter's coming out.

Sexual Abuse

Alas, what shall we do? Sermon by Timothy Palmer

This sermon addresses the gender-based sexual violence in the Congo.

Clergy Sexual Abuse and Misconduct 2010 Sermon by Reverend Lynn Strauss

A minister addresses Catholic and Vatican sexual abuse.

Sermon on Domestic Violence by Rabbi Cindy G. Enger

This rabbi urges congregants to address the problem of domestic violence in all its many forms in their own communities.

"What If No One Had Ever Hurt You?" Sermon by Rev. Debra W. Haffner

This sermon addresses sexual violence, both domestically and abroad.

There are a variety of other times during the year that have been named by secular organizations that might provide another opportunity for addressing sexuality-related issues, especially if they correspond to the lectionary or Torah portions for congregations that use them. This could include services near:

- January 22, the anniversary of the 1973 Roe v. Wade decision on abortion
- February 14, Valentine's Day, Marriage Equality, Standing on the Side of Love
- March, Women's History Month (International Women's Day, March 8)
- April, Prevent Child Abuse Month
- May, National Teenage Pregnancy Prevention Month

- Mother's Day or Father's Day (Sundays can become "wholly family services" which celebrate families of all kinds), Rachel Sabbath Initiative (Maternal Health)
- June, Gay and Lesbian Pride Month
- July 11, World Population Day
- August 26, Women's Equality Day
- September, Comprehensive Sexuality Education
- October, Domestic Violence Awareness Month
- October 11, National Coming Out Day
- November, Family Caregivers Month
- November 20, Transgender Day of Remembrance
- December 1, World AIDS Day
- December 10, Human Rights Day

Clergy can integrate sexuality-related issues into their community's worship life. This could include candlelight remembrance services for people with HIV/AIDS as well as services for people who have had pregnancy losses or have been sexually abused. Congregations may also want to include sexuality-related issues in classes that prepare youth for coming-of-age ceremonies. The congregation can offer celebrations of puberty; ceremonies for divorce, remarriage, and adoption; and services honoring those in middle age (some congregations have had "crone" services for women in menopause) or elders. Baptisms, namings, and dedications can celebrate new life, diverse families, and commitment to children.

Clergy have many hymns, songs, prayers, and responsive readings from which to choose in developing a service or program on sexuality-related issues. A responsive reading and a hymn based on the *Religious Declaration* (available for reproduction and use without permission) are on pages 20–21. The Religious Institute publication *A Time to Every Purpose* also includes responsive readings suggested by each of the Religious Institute's *Open Letters*

including Sex Education, Abortion, Adolescent Sexuality, Assisted Reproductive Technologies, Marriage Equality, Maternal Mortality and Reproductive Justice, and Sexual and Gender Diversity. There are also many scriptural texts that provide opportunities for exegesis on sexuality issues. The box below provides some Hebrew Bible and New Testament texts that may be appropriate for sermons on sexuality-related issues.

SCRIPTURE READINGS ON SEXUALITY
Partial list of texts for worship or Bible study

Genesis 1:1–2:4a (Creation)
Genesis 1:27–28 (Creation, Gender and Reproduction)
Genesis 1:31 (Creation as "good")
Genesis 2:18–24 (Partnership, Gender)
Genesis 2:25 (Bodies)
Genesis 17:11–13 (Culture and Embodiment)
Genesis 29 (Marriage, Pregnancy, Infertility)
Genesis 30 (Infertility, Sexual Consent, Surrogacy)
Leviticus 18 (Culture and Sexuality, Taboos)
Leviticus 19:20–22, 29 (Culture and Sexuality)
Leviticus 21:1–9 (Culture and Sexuality)
Deuteronomy 24:5 (Marriage and Sexuality)
Judges 11:37–39 (Singleness, Virginity)
Ruth 1:1–18 (LGBT, Partnership, and Sexuality)
1 Samuel 18:1 (LGBT)
2 Samuel 1:26 (LGBT)
Song of Solomon (Sexual Pleasure, Marriage)
Isaiah 62:4–5 (Love and the Divine)
Proverbs 5:18–19 (Sexuality and Aging)
Ecclesiastes 3:5 (LGBT issues)
Matthew 19:12 (Sexual Minorities)
Matthew 22: 37–39 (Divine Love, Love for and One Another)
Mark 3:31–34 (Family)
Luke 7:1–9 (LGBT)
Luke 7:36–50 (Expressions of Love, Sexuality)
John 4:16–30 (Marriage, Sexual Boundaries)
John 8 (Culture and Sexual Morality)

A RESPONSIVE READING BASED ON RELIGIOUS DECLARATION ON SEXUAL MORALITY, JUSTICE, AND HEALING

Sexuality is God's life-giving and life-fulfilling gift.

We celebrate our sexuality as central to our humanity and as integral to our spirituality.

We suffer because of the pain, brokenness, oppression and loss of meaning that too many experience about their sexuality.

We celebrate the goodness of creation, our bodies and our sexuality.

We suffer when this sacred gift is abused or exploited.

We celebrate sexuality that expresses love, justice, mutuality, commitment, consent and pleasure.

We suffer because of discrimination against people because of sex, gender, color, age, bodily condition, marital status or sexual orientation.

We celebrate when we are truth-seeking, courageous and just.

We suffer because of violence against women and LGBT people and the HIV pandemic.

We celebrate the full inclusion of women and LGBT persons in our congregation's life.

We suffer because of the commercial exploitation of sexuality.

We celebrate those who challenge sexual oppression and who work for sexual justice.

Together: God rejoices when we celebrate our sexuality with holiness and integrity.

"When Bodies Join and Souls Combine"

A Hymn by Patrick Evans created for the 10th Anniversary of the Religious Institute; based on the Religious Institute Declaration on Sexual Morality, Justice, and Healing.

To listen to the hymn, go to http://ow.ly/aEYsx

CONGREGATIONAL ASSESSMENT ON WORSHIP AND PREACHING ON SEXUALITY ISSUES

Complete this checklist to assess the congregation's strengths and areas of possible growth. Remember that not every area will be appropriate in every congregation. Feel welcome to note "not applicable" or "not now" in the Plans for Improvement area. Discuss with others in the congregation which areas might be improved and the priority for implementing plans.

During the past two years, has there been a worship service or has someone preached on:	Worship		Sermon		Plans for improvement
	Yes	No	Yes	No	
Any sexuality issue?					
LGBT full inclusion?					
Marriage equality?					
Reproductive justice, including abortion and family planning?					
Sexuality education?					
Global maternal mortality? (More resources to celebrate a Rachel Sabbath aimed at education around maternal health can be found at www.religiousinstitute.org/rachel)					
International violence against women? (More resources to celebrate a Congo Sabbath aimed at education around stopping violence against women in the Democratic Republic of Congo can be found at www .religiousinstitute.org/congo)					
Domestic violence?					
Sexual abuse?					
Another sexuality issue?					

Inclusive language	Yes	No	Don't know	Plans for improvement
Is there a policy related to full inclusion language for preaching?				
Does it include:				
Non-gendered words used for the Divine?				
Diverse family formation?				
Partners as well as Husband/Wife?				

In the past two years, have there been:	Yes	No	Don't know	Plan for improvement
Readings on sexuality issues?				
Rite of passage ceremony?				
Celebrations of announcement of a pregnancy or adoption?				
Joys and concerns for the birth or adoption of a child and preparing for marriage or civil union?				
Rituals of celebration for coming out?				
Rituals or celebration to mark transition for transgender individuals?				

Has the congregation participated in:	Yes	No	Don't know	Plan for improvement
Congo Sabbath?				
Rachel Sabbath?				

PASTORAL CARE

Clergy and other pastoral counselors must be prepared and skilled in handling the sexuality-related needs of their congregants. This can include a wide range of issues, such as couples struggling with issues of sexual dysfunction, infidelity, or divorce; people seeking support for the decision to come out as gay or lesbian; families dealing with teenage pregnancy or teen who is coming out; or men and women trying to overcome a legacy of childhood physical and sexual abuse. Every clergy and chaplain can think of times that sexuality issues have been raised in their private offices.

The PLISSIT counseling model is one model that may prove useful for pastoral care providers.[37] It was developed almost 30 years ago for health care providers who are not psychiatrists, psychologists, or sex therapists but who address sexual needs and concerns in their work. PLISSIT is an acronym for Permission, Limited Information, Specific Suggestions, and Intensive Therapy.

PERMISSION means letting the congregant know that it is normal to have all sorts of sexual thoughts and feelings. Permission from clergy to enjoy and accept one's sexual feelings may prove quite powerful for those who have understood their sexual feelings as sinful, bad, or immoral. People can be counseled on the difference between having a sexual feeling and acting upon it, and on the fact that a sexually healthy adult differentiates between sexual behaviors that are life enhancing and those that might be harmful to oneself or others. Permission-giving is not the same as telling someone what to do. It is giving congregants an opportunity to talk about their feelings and their decisions about their sexual behaviors. The clergy's comfort in addressing sexuality issues from the pulpit may also give congregants permission to bring up these issues in counseling sessions.

Clergy are not expected to violate their own religious beliefs or personal values and give permission for behaviors that are counter to them; however, they do have an obligation to first listen and then to be honest with a congregant if their beliefs differ from the majority of sexuality professionals.

In cases of a congregant revealing a history of sexual abuse, each state has different laws protecting the confidentiality of clergy/congregant counseling sessions. As of April 2000, as many as 26 states now require clergy to break a congregant's confidence in order to prevent a serious crime or to report knowledge of child abuse.[38] If congregants reveal beliefs or practices that are harmful to themselves or others (and not just different from one's own), it is appropriate to point out the consequences of those beliefs and refer the person to a professional who specializes in sexuality issues. (See Intensive Therapy below.)

LIMITED INFORMATION involves sharing with the congregant information about the denomination's policies in the area of sexuality, scripture, or church history. Many people incorrectly assume, for example, that scripture teaches that sexuality is bad; pastoral care providers can share scriptural passages with congregants that affirm that sexuality is a positive part of life to be used wisely. LGBT persons may be reassured to know that there is a welcoming movement in their denomination and to learn about resources on positive affirmations of queer people and the Bible. Limited information may also mean providing some information about sexuality, such as anatomy or sexual response, but only if the pastoral care provider is knowledgeable about such areas.

Many people's concerns about their sexuality can be summed up in one question: "Am I normal?" It is important that the congregant understand that the answers to these questions are highly variable and there is no "right answer." Individuals and couples must decide, alone or with their partner, which behaviors, what frequency, and what fantasies are acceptable to them, and whether their sexual decisions and behaviors are congruent with their own values. For every couple, it is appropriate to address such ethical issues as consent, mutuality, non-exploitation, honesty, protection, and pleasure when counseling about relationships.

SPECIFIC SUGGESTIONS means offering simple solutions to congregants about common sexual problems. This is beyond the skills of most clergy and pastoral counselors who might feel uncomfortable discussing the use of lubricants with middle-age couples or start-stop techniques for rapid ejaculation. Nevertheless, they can make specific suggestions to individuals and couples who are seeking more information. Pastoral care providers can recommend specific books or marriage workshops in the area. They can certainly suggest to couples who say they have no time for sex that they set up specific dates or help couples struggling with frequency issues express their needs. They can address the anger and intimacy concerns that frequently appear as sexual desire problems. More directly, they can suggest specific scriptural or denomination policies for reading that may help alleviate a person's guilt and shame about sexuality that may impair sexual functioning and intimate relationships.

INTENSIVE THERAPY is beyond the scope of pastoral care and counseling, not only for sexuality issues but also for mood and anxiety disorders as well as mental health problems. Pastoral care providers know that they need a well-developed referral network of mental health professionals and services in the community. Emergency procedures also need to be in place. It is important to include sexuality, marriage, and family counselors in the referral network. A list of national hotlines that deal with a wide range of sexuality issues is found in the box on page 26. The American Association of Sexuality Educators, Counselors, and Therapists provides a list of certified sex counselors and therapists by state; they can be reached at www .aasect.org or 202-449-1099.

National Hotlines on Sexuality Issues

American Social Health Association's Sexually Transmitted Infections Resource Center Hotline
Hours: 8 a.m.–8 p.m., Monday–Friday, EST
Phone: 800-227-8922

The Centers for Disease Control and Prevention (CDC) National AIDS Clearinghouse
Hours: 9 a.m.–6 p.m., Monday–Friday, EST
Phone: 800-458-5231 TTY: 800-243-1098

Domestic Violence Hotline
Hours: 24 Hours
Phone: 800-799-SAFE (7233)

Emergency Contraception Hotline
Hours: 24 Hours
Phone: 888-NOT-2-LATE (888-668-25283)
www.ec.princeton.edu

National Abortion Federation—Abortion Information, Funding Assistance
Hours: Monday–Friday, 7:00 a.m.–11:00 p.m.,
Saturday–Sunday, 9:00 a.m.–9:00 p.m.
Phone: 800-772-9100
www.prochoice.org

National Abortion Federation—Referrals
Hours: Monday–Friday, 9:00 a.m.–9:00 p.m.,
Saturday–Sunday, 9:00 a.m.–5:00 p.m.
Phone: 877-257-0012
www.prochoice.org

National Child Abuse Hotline
Hours: 24 Hours
Phone: 800-4A-CHILD

National Gay and Lesbian Hotline
Hours: Monday–Friday, 4 p.m.–12 a.m.;
Saturday, 12 p.m.–5 p.m., EST
Phone: 888-843-4564

National HIV/AIDS Teen Hotline, "From One Teen to Another" American Red Cross
Hours: Friday and Saturday
6 p.m.–12 a.m., EST
Phone: 800-440-TEEN

Planned Parenthood Federation of America
Phone: 800-230-PLAN
www.plannedparenthood.org

Rape, Abuse, and Incest National Network: National Sexual Assault Hotline
Hours: 24 Hours
Phone: 800-656-HOPE
Online Hotline: www.rainn.org

RESOLVE: The National Infertility Association
Phone: 703-556-7172
www.resolve.org

Stop it Now! (Preventing Child Sexual Abuse)
Hours: Monday–Friday, 8 a.m.–5 p.m.
Phone: 888-PREVENT

Teens Teaching AIDS Prevention (TTAP) National Hotline
Hours: Monday–Friday, 4 p.m.–8 p.m., CST
Phone: 800-234-TEEN

The Trevor Project: Crisis Intervention and Suicide Prevention Services for LGBTQ Youth
Hours: 24 Hours
Phone: 866-4-U-TREVOR
Live Online Chat: www.trevorproject.org

ASSESSMENT FOR CLERGY AND PASTORAL CARE PROVIDERS ON PASTORAL CARE ON SEXUALITY ISSUES

Complete this checklist to assess the congregation's strengths and areas of possible growth. Remember that not every area will be appropriate in every congregation. Feel welcome to note "not applicable" or "not now" in the Plans for Improvement area. Discuss with others in the congregation which areas might be improved and the priority for implementing plans.

Reporting requirements				
Do you know the state law about when clergy must violate confidentiality to:	Yes	No	Don't know	Plan for improvement
Prevent a crime?				
Report a crime?				
Report child abuse?				
Report child pornography use?				
Protect someone from suicide?				

Training for Religious Professionals				
Have you:	Yes	No	Don't know	Plan for improvement
had training on counseling on sexuality issues in general?				
had training on premarital counseling?				
had training on working with couples with relationship issues?				
had training in divorce mediation?				
taken a course on pregnancy options counseling?				
taken a course on working with sexual abuse survivors?				
Do you know the PLISSIT model for talking about sexuality concerns?				

Have you had specialized training in these areas:	Yes	No	Feel comfortable without additional training	Plan for improvement
Adolescents?				
Bisexual adults?				
Couples counseling?				
Couples affected by infidelity?				
Premarital counseling?				
Couples struggling with infertility or ARTs?				
Disabled persons?				
Families with an intersex child?				
Families with gender variant children?				
Families with LGB children?				
Gay and lesbian adults?				
People involved in alternative sexual communities (i.e., kink, BDSM, online role-playing)?				
People with cognitive disabilities?				
People with HIV/AIDS?				
People with mental health issues?				
Polyamorous individuals/families?				
Transgender adults?				
Young adults 18–24?				

Do you have reading lists to give to congregants on these topics:	Yes	No	Plan for improvement
Adolescents?			
Bisexual adults?			
Couples?			
Couples affected by infidelity?			
Couples during pre-marital counseling?			
Couples struggling with infertility or ARTs?			
Disabled persons?			
Families with an intersex child?			
Families with gender variant children?			
Families with LGB children?			
Gay and lesbian adults?			
People Involved in alternative sexual communities (i.e., kink, BDSM, online role-playing)?			
People with cognitive disabilities?			
People with HIV/AIDS?			
People with mental health issues?			
Polyamorous individuals/families?			
Transgender adults?			
Young adults 18–24?			

Referral Lists / Network

Does your referral list include:	Yes	No	Plan for improvement
Certified marriage and family therapists?			
Certified sexuality counselors and therapists?			
Sex abuse treatment specialists?			

EDUCATION FOR YOUTH

We call for… sexuality education… throughout the lifespan…

────────────────── ℚ ──────────────────

Religious institutions have a unique role to play in reaching children and youth with sexuality information. Religious institutions serve more teens than any other organization in a community except for the public schools, and they are the only ones specifically empowered to teach values to children outside the home. More than half of teens attend religious services and three in four say religion is important in their daily lives.[39]

Participation in a religious setting may in fact protect young people against premature involvement in sexual behaviors. Consider these facts:

- Nine in ten teens say morals and values should play a major role in the decision to have sexual intercourse.[40]

- Teens who report significant levels of involvement in and connection to congregational life and its leaders have the lowest rates of sexual intercourse. Thirty-one percent of faith-involved 17-year-olds have sexual intercourse [41] compared to 62 percent of all teens in the U.S.[42]

- Youth who never attend religious services have more than three times as many sexual partners as those who attend weekly.[43]

- Boys who consider religion very important in their lives are half as likely to have sexual intercourse compared to boys who do not consider religion important.[44]

- Religiously involved teens do have high levels of sexual involvement besides intercourse:

29 percent of these males and 26 percent of these females engage in oral sex; 70 percent in fondling; 50 percent in nudity with the opposite sex; 89 percent of males and 71 percent females masturbate; and kissing is nearly universal.[45]

Yet despite this impact, only four in ten youth agree that their congregation portrays sex in a healthy and positive manner.[46] Disappointingly, but perhaps not surprisingly, 89 percent of youth active in religious institutions say they receive inadequate information on sexual decision-making.[47] One in five teens who are active in their faith communities say that their congregation doesn't do a good job or has done nothing to help them with sexuality issues.[48] Ninety-two percent of leadership in congregations agrees that they could be doing more than they currently are in the area of sexuality education.[49]

Teens and clergy disagree about the sexuality education that is offered. Although 73 percent of clergy said that their congregation portrays sexuality in a positive and healthy way, only 46 percent of the teens in those same congregations agreed. And while clergy and religious advisors rate their sexuality education programs as fair to good, youth in the programs rate them as poor.[50]

The good news is that three-quarters of adults and teens believe that churches and other faith communities should do more to help prevent teen pregnancy.[51] Many denominations have made a commitment to sexuality education for young people. Several have passed policies that encourage their congregations to include sexuality education in their religious education programs. Indeed, more than 40 years ago, the National Council of Churches, Commission on Marriage and Family, the Synagogue Council of America's Committee on Family and the United States Catholic Conference called upon churches and synagogues to become actively involved in sexuality education within their congregations and their communities.[52]

Many denominations have produced sexuality education curricula; the majority are aimed at adolescents. Many are easily adaptable for other faith communities. There are also national organizations that have produced curricula for use in an interfaith setting. (See the box on pages 33 to 41 for a list of religious sexuality education curricula by age level. The Religious Institute provides a regularly updated online bibliography of sex education curricula at www.religiousinstitute.org/bibliography.)

Denominations support very specific types of sex education, consistent with their faith values. Some only support abstinence-only-until-marriage programs, while others are more comprehensive. The Unitarian Universalist Association, the United Church of Christ, and the Union for Reform Judaism have developed their own comprehensive sexuality education curricula which meet the SIECUS National Guidelines for Comprehensive Sexuality Education.[53]

As of 2011, the following denominations have their own sex education curricula:

- Alliance of Baptists
- American Baptist Churches in the U.S.A.
- Central Conference of American Rabbis
- Christian Church (Disciples of Christ)
- Episcopal Church
- Evangelical Lutheran Church in America
- Greek Orthodox Archdiocese of America
- Jewish Reconstructionist Federation
- The Lutheran Church—Missouri Synod
- Metropolitan Community Churches

- Moravian Church
- Mennonite Church
- National Council of Churches of Christ in the U.S.A., Office of Family Ministries and Human Sexuality
- Presbyterian Church (U.S.A.)
- Roman Catholic Church
- Reform Church in America
- Southern Baptist Convention
- Union for Reform Judaism
- Unitarian Universalist Association
- United Church of Christ
- The United Methodist Church
- United Synagogue of Conservative Judaism

Several denominations also support sexuality and/or HIV/AIDS education in public schools. They include:

- American Baptist Church, U.S.A.
- Central Conference of American Rabbis
- Church of the Brethren
- Episcopal Church
- Evangelical Lutheran Church in America
- Jewish Reconstructionist Federation
- Metropolitan Community Churches
- Presbyterian Church (U.S.A.)
- Reform Church in America
- Union for Reform Judaism
- Unitarian Universalist Association
- United Church of Christ
- The United Methodist Church
- United Synagogue of Conservative Judaism

The teachers of sexuality education programs need specialized training in leading the curricula and responding to the sexuality needs of young people. Several of the denominations provide specialized training along with their curricula. If such training is not available, consider using volunteers from within the congregation who already have professional backgrounds and experience working with young people: health educators, teachers, psychologists, and social workers among others.

Good sexuality education programs for young people also include a parent/guardian component. Make sure that there is a session for parents and guardians where they can review the curriculum, meet the group leaders, view the audio-visuals, and have their questions answered. Programs that regularly include homework assignments for children and parents increase parent/child communication about sexuality. Most programs recommend having parents sign permission slips before the program begins.

It may be that adopting a comprehensive sexuality education program, kindergarten through high school, is not yet possible for the congregation. There are less intensive activities that the congregation can offer to support the sexual health and development of teenagers. Consider:

- Using an outside consultant periodically from the health department, local AIDS organization, or local Planned Parenthood to speak with the youth group about sexuality issues

- Facilitating youth group members' participation in community activities that relate to sexuality issues. For example, young people can volunteer at a family planning clinic, AIDS organization, children's hospital, adoption agency, or hotline for young people.

- Providing support groups for young people, including groups for those whose parents are going through divorce, dealing with sexual orientation or gender identity issues, and/or eating disorders and body image issues. Make certain that leaders of "drop in" programs have experience and training handling teen sexuality issues.

- Including pamphlets about sexual health services in the youth center space and hanging posters for young people from such organizations as Sex, Etc., the National Campaign to Prevent Teen Pregnancy, and

Parents, Family, and Friends of Lesbians and Gays (PFLAG). (See the Resources List on page 72 for contact information.)

- Training members of the high school youth group to provide education about peer pressure on dating, drugs, drinking, and sex to the middle school students and pre-adolescents. Modeling safe behaviors will benefit both groups.

- Providing small group sessions or worship services for high school and middle school youth that focus on such issues as body image, peer pressure, relationships with parents, and friendships. Give young people an opportunity to talk among themselves and with trained leaders about the pressures they face.

- Providing a Bible study group for teens that focuses on stories with sexual themes and lessons.

- Offering programs for parents and middle school students on adjusting to the challenges of puberty and adolescence, as well as maintaining communication through the teen years.

- Having movie nights with such themes as relationships, adolescence, marriage, friendships, and sexual orientation. Consider making them intergenerational evenings and facilitating a discussion afterwards with youth and adults.

- Working with youth ministers and religious educators from other congregations to develop community programming.

- Opening youth programming at the church to youth in the surrounding community.

The Religious Institute has published a separate guidebook, *A Time to Speak: Faith Communities and Sexuality Education, Third Edition*, which provides many more ideas and suggestions on sexuality education for children and youth in the congregation. It can be accessed at www .religiousinstitute.org.

SEXUALITY EDUCATION CURRICULA FOR FAITH COMMUNITIES

Many denominations have developed curricula and guidebooks for sexuality education in faith communities.

The following annotated list of materials may help congregations plan sexuality education programs. These materials reflect diverse faith perspectives and diverse values, and most are not appropriate for use in public schools or in every faith community.

This list includes curricula that are still in print. The Religious Institute website includes a regularly updated bibliography of sexuality education curricula. Visit www.religiousinstitute.org/bibliography.

Inclusion in this list does not imply an endorsement by the Religious Institute.

ELEMENTARY

Benziger Family Life Program, Grades K–8
Third Edition
Curricula including teachers' and students' guidebooks for each grade level, kindergarten through eighth grade. There are also an implementation manual and a video for parents. Online program resources include student games, extra activities, official church documents, child development information, and frequently asked questions. Human Reproduction is discussed in the 5th and 6th grade and is primarily focused on providing information. Curriculum recognizes parents as primary teachers. Call for exact prices. (Roman Catholic)
RCL Benziger, 8805 Governor's Hill Dr. Suite 400, Cincinnati, OH 45249; Phone: 877-ASK-4-RCL; Fax: 800-688-8356; Website: www.rclbenziger.com.

Body and Soul Parents' At-Home Guidebook: Nurturing Healthy Sexuality at Home
This publication discusses topics in sexuality through worship and interactive Bible study. It is a guidebook for parents of children ages two through ten and includes a section on practices and habits for promoting healthy sexuality and a list of activities. (Mennonite Church USA)

$8.99; 2010; Faith & Life Resources, 1251 Virginia Avenue, Harrisonburg, VA 22802; Phone 800-245-7894; Fax 877-271-0760; Website: www.faithandliferesources.org.

Created By God: About Human Sexuality for Older Girls and Boys, Grades 5–6
James H. Ritchie, Jr.
A six-session curriculum for older elementary school children emphasizing a healthy biblical and Christian perspective on human sexuality, values, and relationships. There is also a Leader's Resource Kit, which is a step-by-step guidebook to planning and implementing the curriculum. (United Methodist)
2010; Leader's Guide CD-ROM $25; DVD Assistant $25, Student Book $7.50; Cokesbury, 201 Eighth Avenue South, P.O. Box 801, Nashville, TN 37202-0801; Phone: 800-672-1789; Fax: 800-445-8189; Website: www.cokesbury.com.

Family Sexuality Education:
A Course for Parents
Joe H. Leonard
This five-unit program is for parents with children between the ages of three and 12. Topics include: "Exploring and Understanding Our Own Sexuality," "Sexuality Through

Childhood," "Sexuality in the Home," "Values," and "Communication Skills." (American Baptist Church, U.S.A)
1995; $9; Judson Publishing, P.O. Box 851, Valley Forge, PA 19482-0851; Phone: 800-458-3766; Fax: 610-768-2107; Website: www.judsonpress .com.

Learning About Sex
This series of 11 books is designed to help children develop a biblical understanding of human sexuality, and assist parents, teachers, pastors and doctors in answering children's questions. It provides up-to-date and medically correct information, with age-appropriate language and illustrations. In its fifth edition, each level of the series is gender-specific, with separate books for boys and girls (The Lutheran Church — Missouri Synod).
2008; $12.99–$142.89; Concordia Publishing House, 3558 South Jefferson, St. Louis, MO 63118; Phone: 800-325-3040, 314-268-1000; Website: www.cph.org.

Our Whole Lives (OWL): A Lifespan Sexuality Education Series, Grades K–1, 4–6
Part of a comprehensive lifespan sexuality education series developed jointly by the Unitarian Universalist Association and the United Church Board for Homeland Ministries. Material for grades K–1 supports parents in educating children about birth, babies, bodies and families. Following a Parent Meeting and Parent/Child Orientation, the eight class sessions engage children with stories, songs, and activities. In grades 4–6, participants address pubertal changes, read *It's Perfectly Normal*, and examine topics such as values and sexuality, communication and decision-making. Both offer a weekly "Home Link"—a homework project for parents and children to do together. (Unitarian Universalist Association and United Church of Christ)
Call for prices for each level. Unitarian Universalist Association, UUA Bookstore, 25 Beacon Street,
Boston, MA 02108; Phone: 800-215-9076; Fax: 617-723-4805; Website: www.uua.org/owl/main .html.

Preventing Child Sexual Abuse
Ages 5–8 (1994)
Kathryn Goering Reid
Ages 9–12 (1989)
Kathryn Goering Reid with Marie M. Fortune
These two curricula provide information about sexual abuse and prevention. Age 5–8 curriculum offers 10 sessions while the ages 9–12 curriculum offers 13 sessions to be used in Sunday school, Vacation Bible School, or youth meeting settings. (UCC)
1994, Ages 5–8, $13.00; 1989, Ages 9–12, $12.00; United Church Press, 700 Prospect Avenue, Cleveland, OH 44115-1100; Phone: 800-537-3394; Fax 216-736-3713; Website: www .unitedchurchpress.com or www.faithtrustinstitute .org.

MIDDLE SCHOOL/HIGH SCHOOL

And the Two Shall Become One: A Teenage Study-Unit on Sex, Sexuality and the Sacrament of Marriage
Orthodox Church in America Youth, Young Adult, and Campus Ministry
Fr. Michael Anderson, Fr. John Matusiak, Linda Kozler, and David Subu
This seven-session curriculum begins by identifying misconceptions about sex and sexuality; breaking down stereotypes of men and women; and naming sexuality as a God-given aspect of who we are as human beings. The series engages teenagers through discussion, case studies, and role play, and encourages teenagers to ask the Church their questions. Students explore the Orthodox marriage ceremony, discuss a holistic understanding of loving relationships, and commit to their own personal boundaries. (Orthodox Church in America)

Free; available at www.yya.oca.org/TheHub/ StudyGuidebooks/ContemporaryIssues/ TwoBecomeOne/TwoBecomeOne.htm.

Body and Soul Youth Study Leader's Guidebook: Healthy Sexuality and the People of God

This guidebook follows biblical texts with a specific focus on topics that are of particular concern to youth, including body image, attractions, and sexual boundaries. Primarily for high school students, the guidebook can also be adapted to middle school students. Through worship and interactive Bible study, this guidebook explores topics like "Our Bodies, God's Image"; "Created for Intimacy"; "Honoring the Gift of Sex"; and "Holy Desires". (Mennonite Church USA)
$14.99; 2010; Faith & Life Resources, 1251 Virginia Avenue, Harrisonburg, VA 22802; Phone 800-245-7894 Fax 877-271-0760; Website: www .faithandliferesources.org.

Created by God Student Book: Tweens, Faith, and Human Sexuality
James H. Ritchie
A biblically based reference book for children ages 10 to 13. Children will learn what is happening to them physically, emotionally, and sexually—and that sexual decisions are also spiritual decisions. It discusses the changes that are happening as tweens proceed through adolescence including likeness and differences of males and females and a step-by-step guidebook through puberty. DVDs, CDs, and parent guidebooks are available. (Mennonite Church USA; The United Methodist Church)
$7.50; 2010; Abingdon Press, 201 Eighth Avenue South, PO Box 801, Nashville, TN 37202; Phone 800-251-3320; Fax 800-836-7802; Website: www .abingdonpress.com.

Free in Christ to Care for the Neighbor: Lutheran Youth Talk about Human Sexuality
Helen Musik, Dan Jessup, and Crystal Kirgiss
Adapted from the 2006 study "Free in Christ to Serve Your Neighbor," this is a six-session curriculum designed for use with senior high youth. Session titles include: Created as Sexual Beings, The Voices of Influence, When is Sex OK?, Sex, Power, and Abuse, Selling Sex, and Sex for Money. Sessions use current media such as film clips and popular songs to spark discussion. Each session includes a take-home sheet for use by parents that summarizes what was discussed in class with the youth and gives suggestions for conversation started in the home. (Evangelical Lutheran Church in America)
2007; Free; Evangelical Lutheran Church in America; available at www.elca.org/ faithfuljourney/youth.

Girls and Guys (Curriculum Pack)

Two separate, ten-session resources for teenage girls and boys. Designed to be used separately with girls and boys, the sessions address gender-specific issues. Topics for girls and guys include self-perception, purity, sexuality, emotions, and friendship. (Non-denominational Christian).
2002; $12.74 each ($23.98); Youth Specialties, 833 Broadway Suite 201, El Cajon, CA 92021; Phone: 800-776-8008; Website: www .youthspecialties.com.

God's Gift of Sex
Carol Duerksen
From the Fast Lane Bible Studies series, this five-session course is for junior high students. It follows traditional Bible study format with additional skits that address respect for sex role differences, consent, dealing with negative sexual experiences, and how present personal identity affects future sexual happiness. (Church of the Brethren and the Mennonite Church)
1998; $9.99; Faith & Life Resources, 1251

Virginia Avenue, Harrisonburg, VA 22802; Phone: 800-245-7894; Fax: 877-271-0760; Website: www .faithandliferesources.org.

Good Sex: A Whole-Person Approach to Teenage Sexuality & God

Jim Hanckock and Kara Eckmann Powell

A non-denominational Christian based high school sexuality program. In seven sessions, the curriculum covers communication, sexual identity, intimacy, desire, boundaries, and responsibility. The package includes a leader's guidebook ($15.29), with assistance in setting up parent meetings and supplemental activities. The program includes a student journal called "What (Almost) Nobody Will Tell You About Sex" ($8.49) and a 13-segment DVD. This curriculum engages popular culture, uses realistic skits, and provides reflection activities. (Non-denominational Christian)

2001; Youth Specialties, 833 Broadway Suite 201, El Cajon, CA 92021; Phone: 800-776-8008; Website: www.youthspecialties.com.

Healthy Relationship Programs

Jewish Women International

A series of programs for Jewish children and teenagers to examine and talk openly about the dynamics of their social lives, empower them to build healthy relationships, and prevent dating abuse. Jewish Women International offers a number of age-specific programs to build self-esteem and explore relationships through a Jewish lens: girls and boys; 12-year-old tweens to college seniors; students, campers and youth group members; including, Good Guys, Strong Girls, When Push Comes to Shove, and When the Vow Breaks. The length of programs range from one-and-a-half hours to 12 hours. (Non-denominational Jewish)

2009, $50–$75; Jewish Women International, 2000 M Street, NW, Suite 720, Washington, DC, 20036; Phone: 800-343-2823, Fax: 202-857-1380; Website: www.jwi.org.

Journey to Adulthood

LeaderResources

This is an online curriculum for youth from 6th to 12th grade. Youth progress through three levels: Rite 13, Journey to Adulthood (J2A), and Young Adults in Church (YAC). The youth remain with the same group until senior year. The two-year curriculum cycle includes Sunday school and retreat material, parent meetings, movie lists, service projects and fundraisers. The program offers a comprehensive approach looking at self, society, spirituality, and sexuality. Specific to sexuality, the Rite 13 material focuses on gender issues and identity formation, while the high school material focuses on relationships and sexual behavior. The senior high material has two sections titled "Meaningful Is Not Good Enough: How to Decide When to Do It" and "Be Yourself and Stay Alive: Feedback on Sexuality." The material is usually downloaded but can be mailed on CD. (Episcopalian)

Updated yearly; $200 per year for three years (includes resource help); LeaderResources, 38 Mulberry Street Box 302, Leeds, MA 01053-0302; Phone: 800-941-2218; Website: www .leaderresources.org.

Keeping It Real: A Faith-Based Model for Teen Dialog on Sex and Sexuality

This is a seven-session program for ages 13–17, developed by the Black Church Initiative of the Religious Coalition for Reproductive Choice. It consists of a facilitator's guidebook and a teen activity book. The material deals with popular culture, relationships with others, and defining one's personal identity amidst current real life pressures. This is the only curriculum that incorporates direct discussion of racial issues. (Non-denominational Christian)

2000; Free, when trained to facilitate curriculum; Religious Coalition for Reproductive Choice, 1025 Vermont Avenue, N.W., Suite 1130, Washington, D.C. 20005; Phone: 202-628-7700; Website: www.rcrc.org/programs/keepinitreal.cfm.

Learning About Sex

This series of 11 books is designed to help children develop a biblical understanding of human sexuality, and assist parents, teachers, pastors and doctors in answering children's questions. It provides up-to-date and medically correct information, with age-appropriate language and illustrations. In its fifth edition, each level of the series is gender-specific, with separate books for boys and girls (The Lutheran Church—Missouri Synod).

2008; $12.99–$142.89; Concordia Publishing House, 3558 South Jefferson, St. Louis, MO 63118; Phone: 800-325-3040, 314-268-1000; Website: www.cph.org.

Love—All That and More

A program for high school and college youth, it includes a six-session curriculum and three videos, as well as separate facilitators' guidebooks for Jewish and Christian youth. The material focuses on developing healthy relationships that value mutual equality and respect as well as help teens recognize abusive relationships. (Multifaith)

2000; $285; Faith Trust Institute, 2400 N. 45th Street, Suite 10, Seattle, WA, 98103; Phone: 206-634-1903 or 877-860-2255; Website: www .faithtrustinstitute.org.

Love Shouldn't Hurt: Building Healthy Relationships for Jewish Youth
Shalom Bayit

Developed for Jewish youth by Jewish youth, Love Shouldn't Hurt is a dating violence prevention curriculum addressing the age span from middle school through college. Includes Parent Workshop Power Point Presentation CD ROM. (Non-denominational Jewish).

Sliding donation $250–$100; Shalom Bayit: Ending Domestic Violence in Jewish Homes, P.O. Box 10103, Oakland, CA 94610, 510-541-8874 phone; Website: www.love-shouldnt-hurt.org.

Our Whole Lives (OWL):
A Lifespan Sexuality Education Series,
Grades 7–9, 10–12

Part of the comprehensive lifespan sexuality education series developed jointly by the Unitarian Universalist Association and the United Church Board for Homeland Ministries. The junior high and high school curricula include lessons on positive and negative limit setting, development of moral decision-making, addressing disability and sexual identity differences. Further information about the program, planning guidebooks, and advocacy initiatives can be found at the website of the Unitarian Universalist Association. (Unitarian Universalist Association and United Church of Christ)

Call for prices for each level. Unitarian Universalist Association, UUA Bookstore, 25 Beacon Street, Boston, MA 02108; Phone: 800-215-9076; Fax: 617-723-4805; Website: www.uua.org/owl/main .html.

Purity, Virginity, Chastity
Educational Packet (PVC)
North American Council (NAC) of Teen Society of Orthodox Youth Organizations (SOYO)

This resource is a compilation of texts, summary beliefs, questions for conversation about prayers and Scripture that relate to sexuality, moral decision-making scenarios with accompanying discussion questions, and biblical verses that address the Orthodox Church's beliefs, attitudes, and positions about sexuality. PVC encourages teens to dialogue about how the Church's teachings relate to their lives. Topics include the mystery of marriage, birth control, holiness and purity, abortion, homosexuality, co-habitation, and the difference between lust and love (Antiochian Christian Archdiocese of North America).

2010; No charge; PDF available at www .antiochian.org/PVC.

Sacred Choices: Adolescent Relationships and Sexual Ethics (Middle School and High School Modules)
Rabbi Laura Novak Winer
The modules include a facilitator's guidebook, five student sessions, and three sessions for parents. Sessions cover topics such as sexual development, peer pressure, and assertiveness. The curriculum also addresses tough topics such as being "friends with benefits" and "hooking-up". The curriculum is designed to be flexible enough to use with congregations of varying sizes. (Union for Reform Judaism)
2007; $49.95; available from URJ BOOKS & MUSIC 633 Third Avenue, New York, NY 10017; Phone: 212-650-4120; Website: www .urjbooksandmusic.com.

Sex and the Teenager: Choices and Decisions
Kieran Sawyer, S.S.N.D.
The twelve-session curriculum can be used in high school religious education settings. "The program deals with a variety of topics including: what to do on a date; how to tell the difference between love, infatuation, and exploitation; premarital sex; contraception; abortion; adoption and teen parenting; homosexuality; and setting personal moral limits and holding to them." There are suggestions for use on a retreat including games and music selections. (Roman Catholic)
1999; $9.95 Participant Book, $24.95 Leader's Guidebook; Ave Maria Press, P.O. Box 428, Notre Dame, IN 46556; Phone: 800-282-1865; Fax 800-282-5681; Website: www.avemariapress.com.

Sexual Abuse Prevention:
A Course of Study for Teenagers
Rebecca Voelkel-Haugen and Marie M. Fortune
This curriculum for teenagers covers sexual abuse and harassment in six sessions, one and a half hours each, providing information ranging from the facts and myths of sexual assault to media messages about women, men, and relationships. (UCC, Revised and Updated)
1996; $9.00; United Church Press, 700 Prospect Avenue, Cleveland, OH 44115-1100; Phone: 800-537-3394; Fax 216-736-3713; Website: www. unitedchurchpress.org or www.faithtrustinstitute .org.

Some Body!
Steve Ropp
From the Fast Lane Bible Studies series for middle school students, this five-session study helps youth better understand, celebrate and care for their bodies. The units deal with issues of self-esteem, sexuality, physical fitness, and the pressures of alcohol, drugs, and an unhealthy diet from a Biblical perspective. (Church of the Brethren and the Mennonite Church)
1998; $9.99; Faith & Life Resources, 1251 Virginia Avenue, Harrisonburg, VA 22802; Phone: 800-245-7894; Fax: 877-271-0760; Website: www .faithandliferesources.org.

Tough Choices: Bringing Moral Issues Home
Sean Lynch and Brian O'Brien
The curriculum covers eleven specific issues with an appendix addressing another nine issues. The issues range from divorce to drug and alcohol abuse to capital punishment; of particular interest are the sections on abortion, homosexuality, sexuality, child abuse and domestic violence. "Though applicable in several different courses and programs, the basic approach is for a teacher, catechist, or youth minister to assign a moral dilemma to be taken home, read, and discussed using the questions that accompany each." Then each student returns ready to discuss the dilemmas. Information is provided on the official church statements as well as contemporary religious readings. (Roman Catholic)
2003; $19.95; Ave Maria Press, P.O. Box 428, Notre Dame, IN 46556; Phone: 800-282-1865; Fax 800-282-5681; Website: www .avemariapress.com.

True Love Waits 2001: Pure Joy:
God's Formula
An abstinence-only-until marriage campaign for teenagers and college students. Six sessions are designed as an individual study book for personal use or group study. Also available are similar resources: Sexual Resolutions-True Love Waits Resource Book ($3.95), True Love Waits Takes a Look at Courting, Dating, and Hanging Out ($5.95). True Love Waits Goes Home Manual—2003–2004 ($14.95) is a leader's guidebook for use with True Love Waits material. (Southern Baptist)
2001; $4.95 Lifeway Christian Resource, Customer Service Department, P.O. Box 113, Nashville, TN 37202-0113; Phone: 800-458-2772; Fax: 615-251-5933; Website: www .lifewaystores.com/lwstore.

Yad B'Yad: Working Hand in Hand
to Create Healthy Relationships
Iriat Elay
This curriculum, designed to be used by communities from all streams of Judaism, consists of five sessions, complete with text studies, interactive activities and discussion questions. Focusing on the tools needed to build healthy relationships and to prevent dating violence, the course explores issues related to self-esteem, gender roles, healthy friendships and dating relationships, as well as offering strategies for helping those who are involved in abusive relationships. Designed for Jewish youth in the 6th–8th grades. (Non-denominational Jewish)
2005; $24.50. FaithTrust Institute, 2400 N. 45th Street #10, Seattle, WA 98103; Phone: 206-634-1903; Fax: 206-634-0115; Website: www .faithtrustinstitute.org.

You! A Faith that Fits
Irene Elizabeth Stroud
For ages ten to seventeen, this curriculum consists of twelve sessions, covering issues such as community, acceptance, social justice, and

commitment. It includes a session entitled "Soul and Body" that is dedicated to embodiment and sexuality. The session contains four activities, which are broken down by age group, and offers a group exercise with both youth and their parents and guardians to talk about sexuality. Other activities include "And It Was Good," drawing upon biblical passages to affirm the goodness of embodiment, and "Sexuality is More Than Sex," helping participants understand the differences between the terms "sex" and "sexuality." (Metropolitan Community Churches)
2007; $50. Metropolitan Community Churches, P.O. Box 1374, Abilene, TX; Phone: 866-HOPE-MCC. Website: www.mccchurch.org.

LIFESPAN/ADULT EDUCATION

Affirming Persons-Saving Lives:
AIDS Awareness and Prevention Education,
2nd Ed.
William R. Johnson and Cynthia A. Bouman
This curriculum integrates Christian values, Bible study, and theological reflection and prayer into a comprehensive HIV-prevention program reflecting the history of HIV/AIDS and the latest scientific research. It includes eight learning series for each of the following age groups: Preschool/ Kindergarten (four sessions), Grades 1–2 (four sessions), Grades 3–4 (four sessions), Grades 5–6 (six sessions), Youth (11 core sessions and one optional session), Adults (seven sessions), Parents (three sessions), and Intergenerational (seven sessions). Also included are a teacher's booklet, handouts, teacher's support resources, and two videos. (United Church of Christ)
2011; free download; UCC Wider Church Ministries, 700 Prospect Avenue, Cleveland, OH 44115; Phone: 216-736-3217; Website: www.ucc .org/health/hivaids/apsl.

Body and Soul: Health Sexuality and the People of God Series

This series of study guidebooks are each split into four sections that offer opportunities to explore Biblical texts through group reflection and discussion. Through worship and interactive Bible study, church members explore the topics Our Bodies, God's Image; Created for Intimacy; Honoring the Gift of Sex; and Holy Desires. The series includes an Adult Study Leader's Guidebook, Coordinator's Guidebook, Parents' At-Home Guidebook, Worship Leader's Guidebook, and Youth Study Leader's Guidebook. (Mennonite Church USA)

$8.99–$14.99 each (call for pricing on complete set); 2010; Faith & Life Resources, 1251 Virginia Avenue, Harrisonburg, VA 22802; Phone: 800-245-7894 Fax: 877-271-0760; Website: www .faithandliferesources.org.

Breaking the Silence: A Faith Based Model for Adult Dialogue on Sex and Sexuality
Black Church Initiative of the Religious Coalition for Reproductive Choice

A faith-based sexuality education model developed to help adults better address sex and sexuality to assist teens in making healthy life choices. The goal of the nine-session programs is to help participants increase their comfort level talking about sex with teens. The curriculum package includes a leader's guidebook, training modules, bulletin announcements, glossary of terms, information on pregnancy prevention, HIV/AIDS resources, technical assistance, and an extensive biography (multifaith).

2004; Free, when trained to facilitate curriculum; Religious Coalition for Reproductive Choice, 1025 Vermont Avenue, N.W., Suite 1130, Washington, D.C. 20005; Phone: 202-628-7700; Website: www .rcrc.org/programs/breakingthesilence.cfm.

Closer Than A Brother (A Study Series for Men)

A men's study series aimed at men ages 40–60. The series includes 5 books which are designed to help men's groups discuss topics such as sex, family, work, gender roles, and power. One book in the series, Sex and Faith: Celebrating God's Gifts by David Boshart, is designed to help men talk about their questions regarding appropriateness of sexual thoughts and behaviors as well as how men can honor God through their own sexuality (Mennonite).

Faith & Life Resources, 1251 Virginia Avenue, Harrisonburg, VA 22802; Phone: 800-245-7894 Fax: 877-271-0760; Website: www .faithandliferesources.org.

Created in God's Image: A Human Sexuality Program for Ministry and Mission

Overview: Faith A. Johnson and Gordon J. Svoboda, II
Leader's Manual: Eleanor S. Morrison and Melanie Morrison, $12.00
Participant's Book: Melanie Morrison and Eleanor S. Morrison, $12.00 A Manual for Ministry in the Congregation: Mary Ellen Haines and Bill Stackhouse This program is written for college age and adults. (UCC)

1993; Available with training; contact Ann Hanson for more information at 216-736-3282; Division of the American Missionary Association, United Church Board for Homeland Ministries, 700 Prospect Avenue, Cleveland, OH 44115-1110; Website: www.ucc.org.

Free in Christ to Serve the Neighbor: Lutherans Talk about Human Sexuality

This is the third study offered by the Task Force for ELCA Studies on Sexuality under the general theme, "Journey Together Faithfully." The eight study sessions include titles such as: Created as Sexual Beings; Sexuality, Culture, and Freedom; Sexuality and Social Institutions; Sex, Power, and Abuse; Sexuality, Money, and

the Bottom Line; and Sexuality and Economic Justice. Sessions use hymns, prayers, and biblical verse spark discussion. (Evangelical Lutheran Church in America)
2006; Free; Evangelical Lutheran Church in America; available at www.elca.org/faithfuljourney.

Kulanu: All of Us
A Program & Resource Guidebook for Gay, Lesbian, Bisexual & Transgender Inclusion
Richard F. Address, Joel L. Kushner, and Geoffrey Mitelman
This manual offers practical suggestions and curriculum content to encourage gay and lesbian inclusion in the Jewish community. Chapters include: "History and Texts," "Steps to Inclusion," "Life-Cycles," "Leadership Training and Education," "(Re)Defining Family and Temple Membership," and "Employment Practices." (Union for Reform Judaism)
1996; $19.95; URJ Press, 633 Third Avenue, 7th Floor, New York, NY 10017; Phone: 212-650-4120; Fax: 212-650-4119; Website: www.urjbooksandmusic.com.

Our Whole Lives (OWL): A Lifespan Sexuality Education Series
OWL is a comprehensive lifespan sexuality education series developed jointly by the Unitarian Universalist Association and the United Church Board for Homeland Ministries. The series includes OWL Grades K–1, OWL Grades 4–6, OWL Grades 7 – 9, OWL Grades 10 –12, OWL Young Adults Ages 18–35, OWL Adults, A Parent Guidebook, An Advocacy Manual, and accompanying guidebooks on OWL and faith for each grade level. The adult program can be used with adults of all ages or could be adapted for a college audience. Information about the program can be found at the web site of the Unitarian Universalist Association. (Unitarian Universalist Association and United Church of Christ)
Call for prices for each level. Unitarian Universalist Association, UUA Bookstore, 25 Beacon Street, Boston, MA 02108; Phone: 800-215-9076; Fax: 617-723-4805; Website: www.uua.org/owl/main.html.

Talking with Your Teen:
Conversations For Life
Lynn Hutton
One of six chapters focuses on communicating and discussing sexuality with your teen. The section on sexuality can be a helpful addition to youth curricula that do not include a parent section. The curriculum as a whole is a good parent education tool. It includes a leader's guidebook ($10.00) and individual workbooks ($6.00). (United Methodist/Christian)
1999; Abingdon Press, 201 Eighth Avenue South, P.O. Box 801, Nashville, TN 37202-0801; Phone: 800-251-3320; Fax: 800-836-7802; Website: www.abingdonpress.com.

CONGREGATIONAL ASSESSMENT FOR SEXUALITY EDUCATION FOR CHILDREN AND YOUTH

Complete this checklist to assess the congregation's strengths and areas of possible growth. Remember that not every area will be appropriate in every congregation. Feel welcome to note "not applicable" or "not now" in the Plan for Improvement area. Discuss with others in the congregation which areas might be improved and the priority for implementing plans.

Is sexuality education offered for:	Yes	No	Don't know	Plan for improvement
Parents?				
K–1?				
4–6?				
Middle school?				
High school?				
Adults?				

Youth Group	Yes	No	Don't know	Plan for improvement
Do youth leaders know the laws about consent in your state?				
Are youth educated annually about the laws of consent in your state?				
Is there a support group for LGBTQ teens in your congregation or in cooperation with other faith communities?				
Is there a gay/straight youth congregation alliance or one in cooperation with other faith communities?				
Are guidelines for teen sexual and romantic interactions developed each year by the youth group?				
Are these guidelines prominently displayed in the youth group space?				
Are there pamphlets about local sexual health services available in the space where youth meet?				

Do youth-centered or youth-led worship services or education sessions or retreats periodically focus on such sexuality-related issues as:	Yes	No	Don't know	Plan for improvement
Peer pressure?				
Sexual and gender identity?				
Relationships with friends?				
Relationships with parents?				
Safe Internet use?				
Sexual limit setting?				
Abstinence and safer sex?				

Community involvement	Yes	No	Don't know	Plan for improvement
Does the director of religious education have relationships with local youth support agencies for referrals?				
Are there opportunities for youth to volunteer at local community groups that address sexuality issues, such as a local family planning center, AIDS organization, LGBT organization?				

ADULT EDUCATION

Sexuality education is a lifelong process. Our needs for education and information about sexuality change throughout our life. A single 25 year old has different sexuality needs than a 50 year old who is recently divorced and dating again. A couple who has been married or partnered for 25 years has different needs than a new couple planning a wedding. Seniors have needs for different information than those in midlife or those in young adulthood. People with small children have different needs than those whose children have returned to live at home after college.

Current life situation is not the only factor affecting our adult experience of our sexuality. Many adults have experienced brokenness and suffering about their sexuality, often for decades. Survivors of childhood sexual abuse carry issues into their adult lives; for example, 20 percent of women who have been forced to have sex report that they are depressed compared to 12 percent of women who have not.[54] Many adults struggle with issues related to their sexual orientation or the sexual orientation of their children and spouses. Many congregants live in marriages that are experiencing sexual difficulty; estimates are that as many as four in ten couples experience sexual dysfunction and four to ten percent are no longer having sexual relations.[55] Unfortunately, most congregations are silent on these issues, while the people in the pews struggle alone, often without the support of their faith community. But some congregations do offer formalized sexuality education to their adult congregants as part of their adult education programs as well as support groups on a variety of sexuality topics.

There are some denomination resources on adult sexuality education. The Unitarian Universalist Association and the United Church Board for Homeland Ministries jointly published sexuality education curricula for young adults (18–35) and adults. The 12 sessions cover values, communication, sexuality and spirituality, sexual attraction, relationships, love, diversity, family issues, aging, and sexual health. The sessions can be completed in a workshop setting or at a weekend retreat. The framework could easily be adapted for use in other denominations. The Religious Coalition for Reproductive Choice published a nine-week sexuality education program, *Breaking the Silence*, for adults in African-American churches. Its focus is on helping adults work with youth on sexuality issues, but it also includes sessions to "engage African American congregations in a biblical theological and ethnological exploration of human sexuality." Both of these programs could provide a template for the development of an adult education program in a wide range of congregations. A secular curricula, *Older, Wiser, Sexually Smarter* covers mid-life and aging sexuality and could be adapted for a faith based setting. (E-mail The.CFLE@ppgnnj.org for ordering information.)

Many congregations have found that an easy and non-controversial way to begin talking about sexuality in a congregation is to host programs for parents on talking about sexuality with their children. More than eight in ten parents believe it is their job to provide sexuality education to their children, yet few actually do so beyond a few talks in early adolescence.[56] Consider inviting a local sexuality educator with experience in parenting programs to co-lead the group with a religious educator. A single-session course could cover communication with children about sexuality; a multi-session course could cover child sexual development at each stage, parent values, teachable moments, opportunities to talk about faith and sexuality, and communication tips.

Discussion groups about sexuality issues provide another opportunity for adult sexuality education. This can include book groups, which might discuss one of the books listed on page 46 or fiction that deals with sexuality and religion. Consider holding a study group on the *Religious Declaration*. A possible list of questions is found in the box on page 47.

Hosting support groups on a variety of topics is a helpful way to address the particular sexuality needs of congregants. A minister, social worker, or psychologist in the congregation can facilitate support groups. Self-help groups can also be effective: these have no leader but are co-facilitated by people in the group who share the issue in their lives. In the case of a self-help group, the minister, rabbi, or congregation coordinator can identify a time for the meeting, one or two people to facilitate the group, and a place and time, and then post the announcement in the newsletter or bulletin. The group then runs on its own.

There is also an informal sexuality education that takes place in every congregation. Start by thinking about the sex, age, family formation, and sexual orientation of the clergy, director of religious education, the president of the lay leadership committee, the board of trustees, and the Sunday School teachers. Is there gender diversity? Age diversity? Family diversity? Whether one sex gender, age, or marital status dominates certain types of positions or whether there is diversity sends a subtle message about sexuality. Is there a way the leadership of the congregation can become more inclusive and diverse?

Congregations can also more directly provide information about sexuality and local sexual health services. Pamphlets about such topics as contraception, HIV, sexually transmitted diseases, sexual orientation, and gender identity and expression can be in the pamphlet racks in the foyer or social hall. Include pamphlets from community organizations that provide sexual and reproductive health services. Be sure that there are books on sexuality and spirituality in the congregation library. (See the box on page 46 for a core library of books on sexuality and religion.) The congregation can also sponsor a health fair for members of the congregation that includes community-based sexuality services, such as HIV testing and counseling centers, family planning clinics, adoption agencies, sex therapists, and marriage and family counseling.

IDEAS FOR SUPPORT GROUPS ON SEXUALITY ISSUES

- Single adult group or one for each age group (singles 25–35, 35–55, over 55)
- Divorce group
- Survivors of sexual abuse
- Marriage preparation groups
- Marriage/relationship enrichment groups

- Engaged couples
- HIV-positive groups
- Parents of gay, lesbian, bisexual, and/or transgendered children
- Gay and lesbian support groups
- Parents as sexuality educators

A Core Library on Sexuality and Religion, Scripture, and Theology

Religious Institute Study Guidebooks

The Religious Institute publishes study guidebooks on a range of sexuality topics for clergy and lay leaders, as well as reports, monographs, and theological frameworks. Most can be downloaded from the web site, www.religiousinstitute.org/resources. Single copies can be ordered by visiting www.religiousinstitute.org. Information about bulk orders can be obtained from the Religious Institute, 203-222-0055.

A Time to Be Born: A Faith-Based Guidebook to Assisted Reproductive Technologies (2009)

A Time to Every Purpose: The Language of Sexual Morality, Justice, and Healing (2009)

A Time to Heal: Protecting Children and Ministering to Sex Offenders (2005)

A Time to Seek: Study Guidebook on Sexual and Gender Diversity (2007)

A Time to Speak: Faith Communities and Sexuality Education, 3rd Edition (2011)

The following is a list of recent books that can be part of the congregation's library

A La Familia: A Conversation About Our Families, the Bible, Sexual Orientation and Gender Identity by Miguel De La Torre; Human Rights Campaign, the National Gay and Lesbian Task Force, and Unidos, 2011.

All Those Whom God Has Joined: Resources for Clergy and Same-Gender Loving Couples by Leanne McCall Tigert and Maren Tirabassi; Pilgrim Press, Cleveland, OH, 2010.

Body and Soul: Rethinking Sexuality as Justice-Love edited by Marvin M. Ellison and Sylvia Thorson-Smith; The Pilgrim Press, Cleveland, OH, 2003.

Coming Out Young and Faithful by Leanne McCall Tigert and Timothy J. Brown; Pilgrim Press, Cleveland, OH, 2001.

Counseling on Sexual Issues: A Handbook for Pastors and Other Helping Professionals by

Andrew J. Weaver, John D. Preston, Charlene A. Hosenfeld; Pilgrim Press, Cleveland, OH, 2005.

Engendering Judaism: An Inclusive Theology and Ethics by Rachel Adler; Beacon Press, Boston, MA, 2007.

Erotic Justice: A Liberating Ethic of Sexuality by Marvin M. Ellison; Westminster John Knox, Louisville, KY, 2004.

The Erotic Word: Sexuality, Spirituality, and the Bible by David Carr; Oxford University Press, New York, NY, 2003.

Jesus, the Bible, and Homosexuality: Explode the Myths, Heal the Church by Jack Rogers; Westminster John Knox Press, Louisville, KY, 2006.

Just Love: A Framework for Christian Sexual Ethics by Margaret A. Farley; The Continuum International Publishing Group Inc, New York, NY, 2006.

Loving the Body: Black Religious Studies and the Erotic by Dwight N. Hopkins, Anthony B. Pinn; Palgrave Macmillan, New York, NY, 2006.

Ministry Among God's Queer Folk: LGBT Pastoral Care by David J. Kundtz and Bernard S. Schlager; Pilgrim Press, Cleveland, OH, 2007.

Omnigender: A Trans-Religious Approach by Virginia Ramey Mollenkott; Pilgrim Press, Cleveland, OH, 2007.

Sexual Ethics and Islam by Kecia Ali; Oneworld Publications, Oxford, UK, 2006.

Sexuality: God's Gift, 2nd Edition edited by Anne Krabill Hershberger; Herald Press, Scottsdale, PA, 2010.

Sexuality and the Sacred: Sources for Theological Reflection, 2nd edition edited by Marvin M. Ellison and Kelly Brown Douglas; Westminster John Knox Press, Louisville, KY, 2010.

The Sins of Scripture: Exposing the Bible's Texts of Hate to Reveal the Love of God by John Shelby Spong; HarperCollins, New York, NY, 2005.

Their Own Receive Them Not: African American Lesbians and Gays in Black Churches by Horace L. Griffin; The Pilgrim Press, Cleveland, OH, 2006.

Trans-Gendered: Theology, Ministry, and Communities of Faith by Justin Edward Tanis; Pilgrim Press, Cleveland, OH, 2003.

STUDY GROUP ON RELIGIOUS DECLARATION ON SEXUAL MORALITY, JUSTICE, AND HEALING

Consider holding an adult education study group on the *Religious Declaration on Sexual Morality, Justice, and Healing*. Develop a list of questions that the group might use, or adapt the following questions for the group to consider:

- What does it mean that sexuality is one of God's most life-giving and life-affirming gifts?

- How has sexuality been a blessing in your life? How have you experienced your sexuality as broken? How have you experienced it as healing?

- Does the sexual ethic presented in the **Religious Declaration** make sense to you for your own life? How would it need to be modified to become a personal ethic?

- The **Religious Declaration** identifies violence against women and sexual minorities, the HIV pandemic, unsustainable population growth and over-consumption, and the commercial exploitation of sexuality as places where sexuality has caused massive suffering. Decide as a group which of these topics to study in greater depth or have each group member choose a topic to research and present. What are the religious and spiritual issues present? Should your faith community address these issues? What could you do?

- What are your denomination's positions and policies on sexuality issues? Sexual orientation? Sexuality education? Sexual harassment? HIV/AIDS? Abortion? Find and read the statements together. Do you agree with them? Do they go far enough or do they go too far? Is the position or policy reflected in your community life?

1 John 4:19 says: "We love because God first loved us." What are the different types of love in our lives? What role does romantic and sexual love play? Can sexuality be integrated into our love of God?

In 1 Corinthians (6:19), Paul says that the body is a temple. What are our obligations to take care of all the parts of the body, including the sexual parts? What responsibility does society have to see that that is possible?

Discuss what you think the purpose of sex is. Consider this quote:

> If sex is not exclusively, primarily, or necessarily for procreative purposes...then what is it for? If it is for pleasure and/or relational purposes, how can this be articulated in different moral contexts in ways that are women-friendly, safe, religiously faithful, and culturally appropriate across a range of traditions?[57]

Does age matter? Marital status? Sexual orientation? Gender orientation?

What is our responsibility as a community to become involved in sexual justice issues? Is sexual justice only a social action issue or does it have meaning for our life in the faith community?

CONGREGATIONAL ASSESSMENT ON SEXUALITY EDUCATION FOR ADULTS

Complete this checklist to assess the congregation's strengths and areas of possible growth. Remember that not every area will be appropriate in every congregation. Feel welcome to note "not applicable" or "not now" in the Plan for Improvement area. Discuss with others in the congregation which areas might be improved and the priority for implementing plans.

Adult Education Programs	Yes	No	Don't know	Plan for improvement
Are there marriage/couple enrichment programs offered for adults?				
Is there an annual workshop for parents on talking to their children and teens about sexuality issues?				
Is there a periodic adult education offering on sexuality in midlife?				
Is there a periodic adult education offering on sexuality over 65?				
Are there book groups that address books with sexuality topics?				
Are there film or DVD groups that address movies with sexuality topics?				
Are there books in the congregation library on adult sexuality?				
Are there pamphlets about sexuality issues and local sexuality organizations in the pamphlet racks?				
Is there a singles group for lesbian, gay, and bisexual adults?				
Is there a singles group for heterosexual adults?				

Are there support groups for adults facing:	Yes	No	Don't know	Plan for improvement
Histories of sexual abuse?				
Histories of sexual assault?				
Divorce?				
Widows/widowers?				
Coming out?				
Transitioning?				
Families with LGBT children?				
Other?				

WELCOMING AND AFFIRMING CONGREGATIONS

We call for...full inclusion of women and LGBT persons in congregational life, including their ordination and marriage equality.

*I*t is easy to forget that less than 40 years ago, many denominations were embroiled in debates about whether women could be ordained clergy. Although some denominations have ordained women for more than 100 years, many began doing so only in the recent past. The Presbyterians first ordained women in 1965. The first Episcopal women were ordained in the mid-1970s; today, nearly all mainline Protestant denominations ordain women. The first Reform and Reconstructionist women rabbis were ordained in the early 1970s. The first Conservative women rabbis were ordained in 1985.

For many denominations, the controversies around ordination have now largely shifted to gay, lesbian, and bisexual clergy, and, for a few denominations, transgendered clergy. Nearly every mainstream denomination has produced reports on sexual orientation during the past 30 years. Policies range from the "hate the sin and love to the sinner" views of such denominations as the Southern Baptist Convention and the Roman Catholic Church to the full affirmation and acceptance as demonstrated by the national policies and programs of the United Church of Christ, Unitarian Universalist Association and the Union for Reform Judaism. ·

The Unitarian Universalist Association (UUA) voted to "lend full assistance to the settlement of openly gay, lesbian, and bisexual religious leaders" in 1980 and ordained their first transgender clergy in 2000. The United Church of Christ

(UCC) passed a policy that "affirms, celebrates, and embraces the gift of ministry of lesbian, gay, and bisexual persons" in 1991. The Metropolitan Community Churches have been dedicated to providing a religious home for people who are LGBT people since its founding in 1968. Some additional denominations support the civil rights of gays and lesbians and condemn violence and discrimination based on sexual orientation.

With the exception of the few denominations at the forefront of women's equality and LGBT inclusion, most denominations have struggled with the ordination of lesbian and gay clergy, full inclusion of LGBT persons and families, and sacred rites honoring diverse families.

In recent years, several mainline denominations have voted to ordain gay and lesbian clergy. The Episcopal Church ordained its first openly gay bishop in 2003 and in 2009 began allowing its individual dioceses to perform same-sex blessings and/or unions. In 2010, the Evangelical Lutheran Church in America (ELCA) adopted a series of revisions to ministry policy documents to allow Lutherans in committed, publicly accountable, lifelong, monogamous same-gender relationships to serve as ELCA clergy and professional lay leaders. The Presbyterian Church (U.S.A.) voted in May 2011 to remove the requirement that clergy live either in fidelity within the covenant of marriage of a man and a woman, or chastity in singleness.

In other words, Presbyterians who are called to be clergy may now answer that calling, without regard to sexual orientation or marital status. Other denominations are still debating these issues. For example, The United Methodist Church's General Assembly in 2012 included another vote on the removal of a paragraph of current UMC policy that prohibits ordination, certification as candidates, or appointments to serve in ministry of "self-avowed practicing homosexuals."[58]

Several faith traditions do have policies that support the full inclusion of lesbian, gay, bisexual and transgender (LGBT) persons, including ordination and marriage for same-sex couples. These include:

- Alliance for Jewish Renewal
- Central Conference of American Rabbis/ Union for Reform Judaism
- Ecumenical Catholic Church
- Metropolitan Community Churches
- Reconstructionist Rabbinical Association/ Jewish Reconstructionist Federation
- Unitarian Universalist Association
- United Church of Christ
- Unity Fellowship Churches
- United Synagogue of Conservative Judaism

However, many lesbian, gay, bisexual, and transgendered LGBT members do not feel welcome in faith-based communities. In extreme cases, LGBT people and their families have been told they are not welcome or face overt discrimination; in others, homophobia and transphobia are much more subtle. Even congregations that have voted to become open and affirming may hesitate to call an openly gay or transgender clergy person or religious educator.

A sexually healthy faith community welcomes all and includes the concerns of LGBT people at every level of congregational life—in worship, in program, and in social occasions. In the booklet *Taking A New Look*, the authors outline ten reasons that congregations need LGBT people and their gifts. They are:

- The welcome and acceptance of LGBT persons in congregations contributes to a positive image of Christianity, especially among young adults, many of whom have rejected the church.
- Congregations with inclusive attitudes and practices toward LGBT people are much more attractive not only to LGBT people but to many others as well. Becoming a welcoming and accepting congregation can create an atmosphere in which church growth can happen.
- Welcoming and accepting congregations gain the considerable gifts of LGBT clergy, other professional staff, and members.
- Welcoming and accepting congregations become safe places for LGBT youth and for youth who are struggling with their questions about sexual orientation and gender identity.
- Welcoming and accepting congregations make it possible for LGBT persons who are already members to be open about their identity and fuller participants in the life of the church.
- Welcoming and accepting congregations can provide support to families and friends of LGBT persons who have in the past felt unable to safely talk about their questions and concerns.
- Welcoming and accepting congregations are in a better position to offer sexuality education for children, teens, and adults.
- Welcoming and accepting congregations demonstrate the kind of expansive hospitality that God expects of us.
- Welcoming and accepting congregations can stand firmly for human rights and justice not only for LGBT persons but for all people.
- Welcoming and affirming congregations can set people free of the personal distress and even damage to the soul caused by the disconnect some silent friends of LGBT people have between their personal convictions and their public vocalization.

Many faith communities have found it helpful to develop a welcoming committee to begin to educate the congregation on issues related to sexual orientation and gender identity before broaching the possibility of changing policies and procedures. Sessions where people can examine their own attitudes as well as obtain information about sexual orientation and gender identity expression are often helpful. The Religious Institute created *Acting Out Loud,* an online guidebook to LGBT inclusion for faith communities, available at www .religiousinstitute.org/online-guidebook/acting-out-loud. The National Gay and Lesbian Task Force's Institute for Welcoming Resources also provides a toolkit for welcoming LGBT members into congregations, available at www .welcomingresources.org/welcomingtoolkit.pdf.

Many denominations and allied organizations have faith-specific resources on how to become a welcoming and affirming congregation. Almost every denomination now has an organization that is working for full inclusion of LGBT people in congregational life. Many are listed on page 69. The Institute for Welcoming Resources provides an extensive array of resources for Christian congregations on issues ranging from coming out to theological and Biblical resources on sexuality and gender identity (www.welcomingresources.org). The Institute for Judaism and Sexual Orientation at Hebrew Union College Jewish Institute of Religion provides an online learning environment with extensive resources on the intersection of Judaism, sexual orientation and gender identity (elearning.huc.edu/jhvrc).

Congregational Assessment on Welcoming LGBT Persons

Complete this checklist to assess the congregation's strengths and areas of possible growth. Remember that not every area will be appropriate in every congregation. Feel welcome to note "not applicable" or "not now" in the Plans for Improvement area. Discuss with others in the congregation which areas might be improved and the priority for implementing plans.

Worship	Yes	No	Don't know	Plan for improvement
Are we an official welcoming congregation in our denomination?				
Do we provide opportunities for openly LGBT persons (both lay members and clergy) to participate and lead worship?				
Do we publish a statement of welcome in the worship program or bulletin that specifically names LGBT persons?				
Do we name LGBT congregants and raise LGBT issues and concerns in congregational prayers?				
Do we explicitly address issues relevant to LGBT congregants (e.g., marriage equality, nondiscrimination and hate crimes legislation, adoption rights, ordination and other denominational issues) in sermons, education and social action?				
Do we include LGBT people and families in all rites provided for other congregants, such as marriages, baptisms, naming ceremonies, confirmations and funerals?				
Do we challenge scriptural interpretations and religious doctrines that denigrate women, proscribe homosexuality, and promote heterosexism?				

Rituals				
Do we create rituals, prayers or other ways to acknowledge important events in the lives of LGBT congregants, such as:	Yes	No	Don't know	Plan for improvement
A congregant's decision to come out as openly lesbian, gay, bisexual or transgender?				
A congregant's decision to begin gender transition, including the changing of her or his name?				
The celebration of a same-sex couple's anniversary (regardless of whether it is a "wedding" anniversary)?				

The celebration of the adoption of a child, or a co-parent adoption by a same-sex couple of lesbian/gay individual?				
Healing service or prayers for LGBT congregants who have suffered from legalized discrimination, such as denial of marriage or adoption rights, or dismissal from military service?				
Do we observe or mention in any way the following secular events that may involve congregants:				
LGBT Pride Month?				
National Coming Out Day (Oct. 11)?				
Transgender Day of Remembrance (Nov. 20)?				

Education and Visibility	Yes	No	Don't know	Plan for improvement
Do we invite guest speakers to address LGBT social concerns, such as marriage and adoption rights for same-sex couples, hate crimes legislation and homelessness among LGBT youth in our community?				
Do we integrate stories of LGBT lives and the pastoral concerns of LGBT people in ongoing youth and adult education programs?				
Do we include photographs of same-sex couples and LGBT families among other congregants' photos in congregational directories?				
Do we prominently display a rainbow flag on a regular basis?				
Do we make our facilities available for use by LGBT congregational groups as well as LGBT community groups, such as PFLAG, GLSEN and COLAGE?				
Do we provide at least one gender-neutral or "unisex" restroom for transgender individuals?				
Do we provide sensitivity training in pastoral care to LGBT congregants for clergy, lay leaders and other staff, as appropriate?				

Do we include a statement of welcome that specifically acknowledges lesbian, gay, bisexual and transgender people as members of our community, and specifically invites LGBT persons and families to membership on our:	Yes	No	Don't know	Plan for improvement
Website?				
Newsletter?				
Bulletin?				
Congregation signs?				
Congregation brochure?				

Outreach

Does the congregation actively seek LGBT members by:	Yes	No	Don't know	Plan for improvement
Advertising in the local LGBT press, inviting members of the community to visit your congregation for an inclusive worship experience?				
Distributing a flyer on your congregation and its welcoming policy at community centers, book stores, restaurants and clubs that are identified with the LGBT community?				
Hosting an open house for the LGBT community at your congregation?				
Participating with exhibits and tables at local events targeted to the local LGBT community?				
Engaging other clergy in the community in a discussion of theological support for LGBT inclusion and the pastoral needs of LGBT persons?				
Enlisting other clergy and congregations in the community in organizing support for an LGBT issue or participating in a march or other action?				
Utilizing social media marketing to reach LGBT people who may not be familiar with your congregation, such as Facebook and Twitter?				

Other	Yes	No	Don't know	Plan for improvement
Does the religious education program for youth address sexual orientation, beginning with an appreciation of family diversity in the primary grades and expanding to full inclusion in programs for high school youth?				
Are there support groups for LGBT persons and families with LGBT members?				
Is there a program or group for LGBT youth?				
Does the congregation have relationships with local LGBT organizations for referrals and support?				

SAFE
CONGREGATIONS

A sexually healthy and responsible congregation is free from sexual abuse, sexual harassment, and sexual misconduct. Congregations need explicit policies and procedures to keep children, youth, and vulnerable adults safe from abuse and harassment; strong codes of conduct for religious professionals, and safeguards for congregants who have been accused or convicted of sexual offenses.

In too many congregations, people have had their sexuality broken by the very people who minister to them. Tens of thousands of women, men and children have experienced violation by a trusted religious leader in congregations. Sexual relationships between clergy and a congregant, between a pastoral counselor and a client, and between a youth advisor and a teenager are a clear violation of professional ethics, even when the sexual behaviors are consensual.

Although the most publicized cases of clergy misconduct are in the Roman Catholic Church, clergy misconduct has occurred in almost all denominations. It is estimated that 4% of Catholic priests had abused a child sexually between 1950 and 2002[59]. A 2008 study found that more than 3% of women who had attended any congregation in the previous month reported that they had been the object of clergy sexual misconduct at some time in their adult lives. More than 9 in 10 of these sexual advances had been made in secret and two-thirds of the offending clergy were married to someone else at the time of the advance. In the average American congregation of 400 persons, there are an average of 32 people who have experienced clergy sexual misconduct in their community of faith.[60]

At a minimum, a sexually healthy faith community should have written policies on sexual harassment and the prevention of abusive relationships between ministerial and religious education staff and congregants. There needs to be a clear statement that sexual contact, sexualized behaviors, or sexual or romantic relationships by clergy, pastoral care providers, religious educators, and youth leaders with people they serve professionally is a violation of professional boundaries and actionable. There should be written policy on how to file and handle complaints at the local through the denominational level as well as on the services available to the victim and the clergy. Congregations should be aware of denominational or professional resources that are available to help the congregation in the event of a sexual abuse case or sexual misconduct. These policies should be reviewed annually and shared with the congregation through newsletters, bulletins, and annual reports. The United Methodist Church has an exemplary program of policies and procedures on professional sexual ethics and a dedicated website (www.um.sexualethics.org).

There are three key components of a congregational policy on sexual abuse prevention. They are

- Policies and procedures for keeping all children and youth safe from sexual abuse.

- Policies and procedures for educating the adults, youth, and children in the congregation about child sexual abuse and prevention.
- Developing policies and procedures for responding to a person who has been convicted or accused of sexual offenses against children or youth.

Screening for all paid staff and volunteers who work with children and youth as well as developmentally disabled adults is important. The sad fact is that many people who are pedophiles seek work and volunteer opportunities to gain access to children. Many congregations conduct interviews and background checks on all people who work with vulnerable populations. The application form for both volunteers and paid staff can ask if the person has ever used a different name as well as for several years of home and employer addresses. It can also specifically ask such difficult questions as "Have you ever been convicted on any crimes against a person, including rape, incest, sexual exploitation of a minor, sexual or physical assault of a minor?" Such questions and knowing that a police check will occur will likely deter many inappropriate applicants.

Congregations can provide an annual training workshop on issues, policies, and procedures relevant to sexual/physical abuse for all who work with children and youth. They can then ask volunteers and staff to sign a covenant that they will abide by church guidelines forbidding sexual contact or inappropriate verbal exchanges as well as requirements on disclosing abuse to the minister or designated lay leader. Knowing the law in the state about reporting suspected child physical and sexual abuse is essential; having a referral agreement/relationship with the domestic violence and sexual assault programs, as well as sexual abuse treatment providers in the area is also critical as well as support groups for survivors.

Clergy and pastoral care providers also need training to respond to both victims and offenders who come to them for help. When they seek help for past abuse, many people will turn to their minister, priest, or rabbi. Religious leaders can play important roles in helping victims heal and move forward as survivors.

Congregations need to anticipate the potential of a congregant being accused or convicted of a sexual offense. Many people are getting arrested for obtaining child pornography on the Internet. Congregations need policies and procedures to use when a person who is a known pedophile or sex offender wants to be part of the congregation or an existing member is accused of a sexual offense. Congregations must assure that convicted sex offenders do not have the opportunity to reoffend and that they avoid situations where they can be falsely accused. A person with a history of sex offenses may be able to participate in worship or adult education, but should **never** be allowed to be involved in religious education, a youth group, or intergenerational social activities. "The core response of the congregation to a convicted or accused sex offender is a *Limited Access Agreement*. A Limited Access Agreement invites the person with a history of sex offenses to participate in adult worship services, coffee hour, committee meetings, adult education, all-adult social events, and well-supervised intergenerational events. It asks the person to avoid all contact with children on congregation property or at congregation-sponsored events"[61] All states now have sex offender registries where people with a history of a wider range of offenses are listed for the public.[62]

Every congregation also needs education about sexual harassment and a commitment to being a faith community where sexual harassment does not occur. Although sexual harassment is often only thought of as "quid pro quo harassment"— to get a promotion, keep a job, or obtain a valued volunteer assignment sexual favors must be given—it is often actually much more subtle. Unwanted sexual conduct also includes repeated sexual advances, any touching of a sexual nature, graffiti of a sexual nature, sexually offensive gestures, pressure for sexual favors, display or circulation of offensive written materials or pictures, including forwarding emails, unwanted sexual jokes, and talking about one's sexual activity or the sexual activity of others in public.

Teens also need education about sexual harassment. They need to understand that it will not be tolerated in youth group activities. However, it is a mistake to think that only teens harass each other; a clear statement about avoiding such behaviors and a commitment to a sexually safe congregation is also helpful for adult members, particularly around coffee hour and social events. Religious educators, both staff and volunteers, also need this education. Again, the congregation should have a clearly stated grievance procedure for handling complaints of sexual harassment.

In addition, congregations should consider having a clearly stated policy for teen sexual behaviors. Most youth groups do little more than discourage what young people call "PDA," public demonstrations of affection. Yet, such inexplicit pronouncements do not really educate young people. Is handholding allowed? Kissing? Arms around each other? What will happen to young people who go to a retreat and are found engaging in sexual behaviors? Will some sexual activities be forgiven but others punished? A frank, honest discussion each year with the youth group to help them develop standards of behavior to post and share is another sign of the community's commitment to sexual health. Youth group leaders should also be asked to sign a code of ethics that clearly states that they are not to engage in physical or sexual contact, behaviors, or relationships with the teens and youth adults they supervise.

There are a few excellent in-depth resources for congregations on addressing these issues, including the online course *Balancing Acts: Keeping Children Safe in Congregations* by Rev. Debra W. Haffner and Joan Tabachnick www.uua.org/safe/children), A *Time to Heal: Protecting Children and Ministering to Sex Offenders* by the Rev. Debra W. Haffner, and A *Sacred Trust: Boundary Issues for Clergy and Spiritual Teachers* produced by FaithTrust Institute.

CONGREGATIONAL ASSESSMENT ON SAFE CONGREGATIONS

Complete this checklist to assess the congregation's strengths and areas of possible growth. Remember that not every area will be appropriate in every congregation. Feel welcome to note "not applicable" or "not now" in the Plan for Improvement area. Discuss with others in the congregation which areas might be improved and the priority for implementing plans.

Policies				
Do you:	Yes	No	Don't know	Plan for improvement
Have a safe congregations committee or a sexual misconduct and abuse response team with primary responsibilities for these issues?				
Have a written policy on safe congregations?				
Have written overall policies and procedures specifically on preventing sexual harassment?				
Is the safe congregation policy:				
Posted on the website?				
Run in the newsletter once annually?				
Included in new members materials?				
Posted on a bulletin board?				

Is the sexual harassment policy:	Yes	No	Don't know	Plan for improvement
Posted on the website?				
Run in the newsletter once annually?				
Included in new members' materials?				
Posted on a bulletin board?				

Reporting and Screening	Yes	No	Don't know	Plan for improvement
Do you make sure that the minister, the religious educator, and the board chair know the state laws for reporting concerns about abuse to children?				
Do all volunteers in the religious education program receive annual training on what to do if they suspect child abuse or child sexual abuse?				
Do you have a screening form for all employees, regardless of position?				
Do you have a screening form for all volunteers who work with children and youth asking them directly about possible histories of sexual offenses?				

Sexual Offenders	Yes	No	Don't know	Plan for improvement
Do you have a draft of a limited access agreement or checklist for convicted or accused sex offenders?				
Do you have a written policy in place for a process for responding to an allegation of sexual abuse:				
Against a member?				
Against a visitor?				
Against a staff person?				
Against a sexual offender recently released on probation?				

Education	Yes	No	Don't know	Plan for improvement
Do you include education about child sexual abuse prevention in the religious education program at least twice during elementary school?				
Once during middle school?				
And once for your teen group?				

	Yes	No	Don't know	Plan for improvement
Do you hold an annual adult education program on sexual abuse prevention for parents and families?				
Do you have two adults present in each class or program for children and youth?				
Do you have two unrelated adults required for cars transporting young people to activities?				

Babysitters

Do teens and young adults who babysit at church functions:	Yes	No	Don't know	Plan for improvement
Fill out the screening form?				
Receive training on sexual abuse identification and prevention?				
Receive encouragement in writing and in a course to speak with minister or DRE if they have a history of sexual abuse?				
Understand two teens must be present at all times with younger children?				
Do you prohibit babysitters at church functions who have not been screened and educated about sexual abuse?				

Pastoral Care	Yes	No	Don't know	Plan for improvement
Do you make sure the minister has a referral list of community organizations and therapists who specialize in sex abuse prevention and treatment in case you need them?				
Do you have support groups available to those who have survived child sexual abuse?				
Do you offer pastoral care for those who have survived child sexual abuse?				

SOCIAL ACTION/ OUTREACH

Faith communities must also advocate for sexual and spiritual wholeness in society. We call for:

- *Lifelong, age appropriate sexuality education in schools, seminaries, and community settings.*

- *A faith-based commitment to sexual and reproductive rights, including access to voluntary contraception, abortion, and HIV/STD prevention and treatment.*

- *Religious leadership in movements to end sexual and social injustice.*

Almost all faith communities have strong traditions of community service and involvement in social action. The *Religious Declaration* calls on faith communities to offer prophetic witness for sexual justice in the society as a whole; this could include advocating for sexuality education in schools and community agencies, working for access to sexual and reproductive health services, and helping to end discrimination and violence against women and LGBT persons. Not every congregation will be ready to speak out on sexuality issues, but most congregations could become involved in community health and education activities. As the congregation pays attention to its own sexual health, it will become easier to address the sexuality needs of the larger community.

Involvement in social action on sexual justice issues can help the congregation:

- Demonstrate support for all people in the community, not just the people in the congregation.
- Make visible the congregation's commitment to social and sexual justice. Increase the congregation's visibility and influence in the community.
- Provide an opportunity to work with other like-minded faith communities.
- Engage individual member involvement in the community.
- Provide a forum for community-wide partnerships.

Perhaps most importantly, involvement in social action on behalf of sexual justice provides a visible demonstration that there are many religious points of view on sexuality issues.

Too often, only the viewpoints of highly conservative faith leaders are present in community controversies on sexuality issues. The media often only includes this point of view in discussions of such issues as the morality of abortion, gay rights, and sexuality education, pitting a faith leader from a conservative tradition against a secular voice from the mainstream.

Yet most people of faith support sexual rights. For example, in recent polls, 76% of Jews, 55% of mainline Protestants,[63] and 51% of Roman Catholics support legal abortion, at least in some circumstances.[64] A majority of people of faith support marriage or civil unions for same-sex couples.

Active involvement by clergy and people of faith who support sexual justice is essential to assuring that all religious voices are heard and considered. So is the involvement of the laity in these issues. Many conservative faith communities have active and visible public roles when such issues as sexuality education, sexual rights for LGBT people, and reproductive justice are debated. But mainstream and progressive congregation members are often not present.

A congregation can begin by researching the denomination's policies on sexuality issues. Many denominations have developed policies on reproductive choice, sexuality education, HIV/AIDS, and sexual orientation. Depending on the denomination's position on polity, these positions may be binding on the congregation or there may be an opportunity to ratify or modify them for the congregation. Consider using the bulletin or newsletter to reprint these positions for your members. Consider bringing these issues to a congregational vote, if appropriate. The Religious Institute maintains a database of denominations on 20 sexuality issues; it is updated regularly and can be found at www.religiousinstitute.org/denominational-statements.

Some congregations have chosen to vote to endorse the *Religious Declaration* as a sign of their commitment to sexual justice and health or to create their own policy position. It then becomes the congregation's value statement on sexuality issues. Copies can be posted on bulletin boards, inserted into congregational handbooks, periodically run in the bulletin or newsletter, or given to new members.

Social action committees may want to encourage congregants to join the Religious Institute's Faithful Voices Network. Members of the Faithful Voices Network sign a simple pledge, "*As a person of faith, I support sexual health, education and justice,*" and receive monthly emails on breaking issues. Sign up at: religiousinstitute.org/faithfulvoices.

The social action committee can conduct a variety of activities in support of sexual justice.

They can:

- Conduct letter/email writing campaigns on behalf of legislation that is pending at the local, state, or national level on these issues.
- Hold community forums on emerging issues. Participate in school board meetings, state legislative hearings, community rallies, and the like.
- Develop a bulletin board on sexual justice issues in the foyer or meeting room.
- Encourage the clergy to appear in the electronic media, speaking on behalf of a progressive religious view on sexuality.
- Write Op-Ed pieces for the local newspaper or cable station.

Staying up-to-date on emerging sexual justice issues is time-consuming, but there are national organizations with websites and social media that can help.

- The Religious Institute publishes a monthly e-newsletter and maintains an online clearinghouse of information on religion and the issues of sexuality education, reproductive justice, LGBT inclusion, abuse prevention, and international sexual and reproductive health. Visit www.religiousinstitute.org to learn more and endorse its *Open Letters* and *Religious Declaration* at www.religiousinstitute.org/endorse. Follow the Religious Institute on Twitter @ReligiousInst and on Facebook at www.facebook.com/ReligiousInstitute. Sign up for the newsletter list at www.religiousinstitute/faithfulvoice.
- FaithTrust Institute sends out an e-newsletter on domestic violence and misconduct prevention and has an array of resources available on their website: faithtrustinstitute.org.
- GLAAD has a weekly Religion, Faith and Values Newsletter, which highlights the latest in LGBT faith news. Individuals can subscribe by sending an email to faith@glaad.org with the subject line "subscribe" (www.glaad.org).
- The Human Rights Campaign's Religion and Faith program publishes resources, such as

an online weekly preaching and devotional resource, *Out In Scripture,* and a biweekly e-newsletter. Learn more on their website: www.hrc.org/scripture.

- Many Voices: Sharing Ways to Welcome in Faith empowers Protestant pastors and church members to include and affirm LGBT people. They send out a regular e-mail update (www.manyvoices.org).

- People for the American Way's African American Religious Affairs leadership program sends out regular updates. Interested individuals can sign up for this service at www .pfaw.org/leadership-programs/aara/signup.

- SIECUS (Sexuality Information and Education Council of the United States) sends e-mails with regular updates and special reports on sexuality education issues in the United States (www.siecus.org).

- SisterSong: Women of Color Reproductive Justice Collective sends e-alerts (www .sistersong.net).

- The Guttmacher Institute has a series of e-mail newsletters and listservs on a variety of domestic and international reproductive health issues. Individuals can choose which they would like to subscribe to at www .guttmacher.org/listserv/index.html.

- The Institute for Welcoming Resources' website has many LGBT welcoming and inclusion resources for a variety of faith communities and keeps its visitors well informed of current events. Visit their website at www.welcomingresources.org.

- The National Black Justice Coalition is a civil rights organization dedicated to empowering Black LGBT people. The organization sends out a monthly e-digest (www.nbjc.org).

- The National Latina Institute for Reproductive Health sends out a monthly newsletter as well as action alerts (latinainstitute.org).

- The Religious Coalition for Reproductive Choice maintains a useful website (rcrc .org) with information on different religious traditions and reproductive justice. Find them on Twitter, @RCRChoice, and on Facebook at www.facebook.com/pages/ Religious-Coalition-for-Reproductive-Choice.

- TransFaith has an email update list that provides occasional news and information about faith and transgender issues (www .transfaithonline.org).

See the Resource List on pages 70 to 72 for more information on these and other organizations.

CONGREGATIONAL ASSESSMENT ON SOCIAL ACTION FOR SEXUAL JUSTICE

Complete this checklist to assess the congregation's strengths and areas of possible growth. Remember that not every area will be appropriate in every congregation. Feel welcome to note "not applicable" or "not now" in the Plan for Improvement area. Discuss with others in the congregation which areas might be improved and the priority for implementing plans.

Is the minister or a key lay leader a member of:	Yes	No	Don't know	Plan for improvement
Planned Parenthood Federation of America's Clergy Action Board?				
State or local boards of family planning agencies, HIV/AIDS centers, LGBT community agencies?				
Religious Coalition for Reproductive Choice?				
Religious Institute network?				
Human Rights Campaign Faith and Religion Program?				

Congregation Policies				
Do you have congregation policies on:	Yes	No	Don't know	Plan for improvement
Sexuality education in schools?				
HIV/AIDS?				
Sexual orientation?				
Gender orientation?				
Reproductive choice/justice?				
Are these positions periodically included in the newsletter or bulletin?				
Is there a copy of the Religious Declaration prominently posted?				

Advocacy	Yes	No	Don't know	Plan for improvement
Do we advocate for sexuality education in our community's public schools?				
Do we hold community forms on sexual justice issues? How often and on what issues?				
Is there a bulletin board devoted to sexual justice issues?				

Are letter-writing campaigns conducted on sexual justice issues at the:	Yes	No	Don't know	Plan for improvement
Local level?				
State level?				
National level?				

Do members of the congregation participate in:	Yes	No	Don't know	Plan for improvement
School board meetings?				
State legislative hearings?				
Community rallies?				

Minister	Yes	No	Don't know	Plan for improvement
Does the minister periodically give sermons that include prophetic witness on sexual justice issues?				
Does the lay leadership encourage the minister to appear in the local electronic and print media?				
Is the minister an endorser of the Religious Declaration?				
Does the minister or key lay leader blog/ tweet/or Facebook post on these issues?				
Does the minister raise sexual justice issues with diverse faith leaders at such venues as community clergy associations?				

Congregant Involvement	Yes	No	Don't know	Plan for improvement
Do we encourage our congregants to join the Religious Institute's Faithful Voices Network?				
Are there letter-writing campaigns or tables on sexual justice issues?				
Does the congregation hold community forums on sexual justice issues?				

DENOMINATIONS SUPPORT SEXUAL JUSTICE

Sexuality Education

The following denominational bodies have policies supporting sexuality and/or HIV/AIDS education in public schools:

- American Baptist Church, U.S.A.
- Central Conference of American Rabbis
- Church of the Brethren
- Episcopal Church
- Evangelical Lutheran Church in America
- Jewish Reconstructionist Federation
- Metropolitan Community Churches
- Presbyterian Church (U.S.A.)
- Reform Church in America
- Union for Reform Judaism
- Unitarian Universalist Association
- United Church of Christ
- The United Methodist Church
- United Synagogue of Conservative Judaism

Other religious organizations that support sexuality and/or HIV/AIDS education in public schools include:

- American Jewish Congress, Commission on Women's Equality Central Conference of American Rabbis
- Americans United for Separation of Church and State
- Balm in Gilead
- Catholics for Choice
- Friends Seminary
- Hadassah
- Jewish Women International
- National Committee for Public Education and Religious Liberty
- National Council of Churches of Christ in the U.S.A, Office of Family Ministries and Human Sexuality

- National Council of Jewish Women
- Network of Spiritual Progressives
- Presbyterians Affirming Reproductive Options
- Protestants for the Common Good
- Religious Action Center of Reform Judaism
- The Shalom Center
- Women's Alliance for Theology, Ethics, and Ritual
- Women of Reform Judaism
- Women's League for Conservative Judaism
- Young Women's Christian Association of the United States

Reproductive Justice

The following religious denominations have passed policies in support of legal abortion:

- American Baptist Churches in the USA
- Christian Church (Disciples of Christ)
- Episcopal Church
- Evangelical Lutheran Church in America
- Jewish Reconstructionist Federation
- Moravian Church-Northern Province
- Presbyterian Church (U.S.A.)
- Union for Reform Judaism
- Unitarian Universalist Association
- United Church of Christ
- The United Methodist Church
- United Synagogue of Conservative Judaism

The following religious denominations and institutions have policies or programs that support the Millennium Development Goals and/or international family planning:

- American Baptist Churches USA
- Christian Church (Disciples of Christ)
- Episcopal Church

- Evangelical Lutheran Church in America
- Metropolitan Community Churches
- National Council of the Churches of Christ in the USA
- Presbyterian Church (U.S.A.)
- United Church of Christ
- The United Methodist Church
- Union for Reform Judaism
- Unitarian Universalist Association

LGBT Full Inclusion

The following religious traditions have policies that support full inclusion of lesbian and gay persons, including ordination and marriage for same-sex couples:

- Central Conference of American Rabbis / Union for Reform Judaism
- Metropolitan Community Churches
- Reconstructionist Rabbinical Association / Jewish Reconstructionist Federation
- Unitarian Universalist Association
- United Church of Christ
- Unity Fellowship Churches

The following denominations ordain openly lesbian, gay and bisexual clergy members:

- Central Conference of American Rabbis*
- Episcopal Church USA
- Evangelical Lutheran Church in America
- Jewish Reconstructionist Federation / Reconstructionist Rabbinical Association
- Metropolitan Community Churches*
- Presbyterian Church (U.S.A.)
- Unitarian Universalist Association*
- United Church of Christ*
- Unity Fellowship Churches
- United Synagogue for Conservative Judaism

* Also ordains openly transgender clergy.

The following religious groups, while they may not be sponsored by their denomination, are working for sexual justice for LGBT persons.

- Affirmation: Gay and Lesbian Mormons
- Al-Fatiha (LGBT Muslims)
- Association of Welcoming and Affirming Baptists
- Brethren Mennonite Council for LGBT Interests
- Dignity U.S.A (Catholic)
- Evangelicals Concerned
- Gay and Lesbian Acceptance: GALA (Community of Christ)
- Gay Lesbian + Affirming Disciples (GLAD) Alliance
- Alliance (Disciples)
- Institute for Welcoming Resources
- Integrity USA (Episcopal)
- Keshet (Jewish)
- Kinship International (Seventh-Day Adventists)
- Lutherans Concerned
- More Light Presbyterians
- Nehirim: LGBT Jewish Culture and Spirituality
- Open and Affirming United Church of Christ
- Reconciling Ministries Network (Methodist)
- Room for All (Reformed Church in America)
- Soulforce, Inc.
- Standing on the Side of Love (Unitarian Universalist)
- Welcoming Community Network (Community of Christ)

RESOURCES

SEXUALLY HEALTHY AND RESPONSIBLE SEMINARIES

As of December 2012, the following seminaries meet at least two thirds of the criteria for a sexually healthy and responsible seminary.

- Andover Newton Theological School
- Bangor Theology Seminary
- Brite Divinity School
- Candler School of Theology
- Chicago Theological Seminary
- Claremont School of Theology
- Drew Theological School
- Episcopal Divinity School
- Harvard Divinity School
- Hebrew Union College, Jewish Institute of Religion, New York
- Jewish Theological Seminary
- Meadville Lombard Theological School
- Pacific School of Religion
- Reconstructionist Rabbinical College
- Starr King School for the Ministry
- Union Theological Seminary in the City of New York
- University of Chicago Divinity School
- Vanderbilt University Divinity School
- Wake Forest University Divinity School
- Yale Divinity School

SEXUALITY AND RELIGION — ALL AREAS

RELIGIOUS INSTITUTE
21 Charles Street, Suite 140
Westport, CT 06880
203-222-0055
www.religiousinstitute.org

WOMEN'S ALLIANCE FOR THEOLOGY, ETHICS AND RITUAL (WATER)
8121 Georgia Avenue, Suite 310
Silver Spring, MD 20910
301-589-2509
www.hers.com/~water/

HIV/AIDS

THE BALM IN GILEAD
701 East Franklin Street, Suite 1000
Richmond, VA 23219
804-644-2256 (BALM)
www.balmingilead.org

GLOBAL AIDS
INTERFAITH ALLIANCE
The Presidio of San Francisco
P.O. Box 29110
San Francisco, CA, 94129
415-461-7196
www.thegaia.org

REPRODUCTIVE JUSTICE

CATHOLICS FOR CHOICE
1436 U Street NW, Suite 301
Washington, DC 20009
202-986-6093
www.catholicsforchoice.org

CHOICE USA
1317 F Street NW, Suite 501
Washington, DC 20004
888-784-4494
www.choiceusa.org

GENERATIONS AHEAD
405 14th Street, Suite 605
Oakland, CA 94612
510-832-0852
www.generations-ahead.org

NARAL PRO-CHOICE AMERICA
1156 15th Street NW, Suite 700
Washington, DC 20005
202-973-3000
www.naral.org

NATIONAL LATINA INSTITUTE FOR REPRODUCTIVE HEALTH
50 Broad Street, Suite 1937
New York, NY 10004
Phone: 212-422-2553
www.latinainstitute.org

PLANNED PARENTHOOD FEDERATION OF AMERICA (PPFA)
434 West 33rd Street
New York, NY 10001
212-541-7800
www.ppfa.org

RELIGIOUS COALITION FOR
REPRODUCTIVE CHOICE (RCRC)
1413 K Street NW
Washington, DC 20005
202-628-7700
www.rcrc.org

SISTERSONG: WOMEN OF
COLOR REPRODUCTIVE JUSTICE
COLLECTIVE
1237 Ralph David Abernathy
    Boulevard SW
Atlanta, GA 30310
404-756-2680
www.sistersong.net

SEXUAL ABUSE

FAITHTRUST INSTITUTE
2400 N. 45th Street, Suite 101
Seattle, WA 98103
206-634-1903
www.faithtrustinstitute.org

THE SEXUAL ETHICS TASK
FORCE OF THE UNITED
METHODIST CHURCH
General Commission on
    the Status and Role of Women
77 W. Washington Street, Suite 1009
Chicago, IL 60602
312-346-4900
www.umsexualethics.org

STOP IT NOW!
351 Pleasant Street, Suite B-319
Northampton, MA 01060
413-587-3500
www.stopitnow.org

SOCIAL ACTION

AMERICANS UNITED FOR
SEPARATION OF CHURCH
AND STATE
1301 K Street NW, Suite 850,
    East Tower
Washington, DC 20005
202-466-3234
www.au.org

THE INTERFAITH ALLIANCE
1212 New York Avenue NW,
    Suite 1250
Washington, DC 20005
800-510-0969
www.interfaithalliance.org

WELCOMING AND
AFFIRMING ORGANIZATIONS

AFFIRMATION: GAY AND
LESBIAN MORMONS
P.O. Box 1435
Palm Springs, CA 92263
661-267-2421
www.affirmation.org

BELIEVE OUT LOUD
274 Fifth Avenue
New York, NY 10001
www.believeoutloud.com

BRETHREN MENNONITE COUNCIL
FOR LGBT INTERESTS
P.O. Box 6300
Minneapolis, MN 55406
612-343-2060
www.bmclgbt.org

CENTER FOR LESBIAN AND
GAY STUDIES IN RELIGION
AND MINISTRY
Pacific School of Religion
1798 Scenic Avenue
Berkeley, CA 94709
510-849-8206
www.clgs.org

DIGNITY USA
P.O. Box 376
Medford, MA 02155
800-877-9797
www.dignityusa.org

GALA (COMMUNITY OF CHRIST)
P.O. Box 2173
Independence, MO 64055
816-616-5883
www.galaweb.org

GAY LESBIAN + AFFIRMING
DISCIPLES (GLAD) ALLIANCE, INC.
P.O. Box 44400
Indianapolis, IN 46244
703-866-4628
www.gladalliance.org

GAY AND LESBIAN ALLIANCE
AGAINST DEFAMATION (GLAAD)
104 West 29th Street, 4th Floor
New York, NY 10001
212-629-3322
www.glaad.org

FELLOWSHIP OF
AFFIRMING MINISTRIES
www.radicallyinclusive.com

FREEDOM TO MARRY
116 West 23rd Street, Suite 500
New York, NY 10011
212-851-8418
www.freedomtomarry.org

HUMAN RIGHTS CAMPAIGN (HRC):
RELIGION AND FAITH PROGRAM
1640 Rhode Island Avenue NW
Washington, DC 20036
202-628-4160
www.hrc.org

INSTITUTE FOR WELCOMING
RESOURCES OF THE NGLTF
122 Franklin Avenue W, Suite 210
Minneapolis, MN 55404
612-821-4397
www.welcomingresources.org

INTEGRITY, USA
838 East High Street, #291
Lexington, KY 40502
800-462-9498
www.integrityusa.org

LUTHERANS CONCERNED
P.O. Box 4707
Saint Paul, MN 55104
651-665-0861
www.lcna.org

MANY VOICES: SHARING
WAYS TO WELCOME IN FAITH
www.manyvoices.org

METROPOLITAN
COMMUNITY CHURCHES
P.O. Box 1374
Abilene, TX 79604
310-360-8640
www.mccchurch.org

MORE LIGHT PRESBYTERIANS
4737 County Road 101, PMB #246
Minnetonka, MN 55345
505-820-7082
www.mlp.org

NATIONAL CENTER FOR
TRANSGENDER EQUALITY (NCTE)
1325 Massachusetts Avenue NW,
    Suite 700
Washington, DC 20005
202-903-0112
www.transequality.org

NATIONAL GAY AND LESBIAN
TASK FORCE (NGLTF)
National Religious
    Leadership Roundtable
1325 Massachusetts Avenue NW,
    Suite 600
Washington, DC 20005
202-393-5177
www.thetaskforce.org

OFFICE OF BISEXUAL, GAY,
LESBIAN, AND TRANSGENDER
MINISTRIES, UNITARIAN
UNIVERSALIST ASSOCIATION
25 Beacon Street
Boston, MA 02108
617-948-6461
www.uua.org

PARENTS, FAMILIES, AND
FRIENDS OF LESBIANS AND GAYS
TRANSGENDER NETWORK (PFLAG)
PFLAG National Office
1828 L Street, NW
Washington, DC 20036
202-467-8180
www.pflag.org

RECONCILING
MINISTRIES NETWORK
3801 N. Keeler Avenue
Chicago, IL 60641
773-736-5526
www.rmnnetwork.org

SEVENTH-DAY ADVENTIST
KINSHIP INTERNATIONAL
P.O. Box 69
Tillamook, OR 97141
www.sdakinship.org

SOULFORCE
P.O. Box 2499
Abilene, TX 79604
888-326-5610
www.soulforce.org

STANDING ON THE
SIDE OF LOVE
25 Beacon Street
Boston, MA 02108
202-393-2255
www.standingonthesideoflove.org

UNITED CHURCH OF
CHRIST COALITION FOR
LGBT CONCERNS
2592 West 14th Street
Cleveland, OH 44113
800-653-0799
www.ucccoalition.org

WELCOMING AND
AFFIRMING BAPTISTS
P.O. Box 2595456
Kensington, MD 20895
240-242-9220
www.wabaptists.org

YOUTH ISSUES/SEXUALITY EDUCATION

ADVOCATES FOR YOUTH
2000 M Street NW, Suite 750
Washington, DC 20036
202-419-3420
www.advocatesforyouth.org

ANSWER/SEX ETC.
Center for Applied Psychology
Rutgers University
41 Gordon Road, Suite C
Piscataway, NJ 08854
732-445-7929
answer.rutgers.edu

GUTTMACHER INSTITUTE
125 Maiden Lane, 7th floor
New York, NY 10038
212-248-1111
www.guttmacher.org

NATIONAL CAMPAIGN
TO PREVENT TEEN PREGNANCY
1776 Massachusetts Avenue, NW,
    Suite 200
Washington, DC 20036
202-478-8500
www.thenationalcampaign.org

SEXUALITY INFORMATION AND
EDUCATION COUNCIL OF THE
UNITED STATES (SIECUS)
1706 R Street, NW
Washington, DC 20009
202-265-2405
www.siecus.org

* NOTE: If you know of other
organizations that should be
included in this list, please
e-mail the Religious Institute at
info@religiousinstitute.org.

ABOUT THE RELIGIOUS INSTITUTE, INC.

Founded in 2001, the Religious Institute is a national, multifaith organization dedicated to promoting sexual health, education and justice in faith communities and society. The Religious Institute partners with clergy and congregations, denominations, seminaries, national advocacy organizations, and sexual and reproductive health communities to promote:

- Sexually healthy faith communities
- Full equality of women and of lesbian, gay, bisexual and transgender persons in congregations and communities
- Marriage equality
- Comprehensive sexuality education
- Reproductive justice
- A responsible approach to adolescent sexuality
- Sexual abuse prevention
- HIV/AIDS education and prevention
- Global maternal health

The mission of the Religious Institute is to develop a new understanding of the relationship between religion and sexuality. This mission involves:

- Developing and supporting a network of clergy, religious educators, theologians, ethicists and other religious leaders committed to sexual justice.
- Building the capacity of religious institutions and clergy to provide sexuality education within the context of their faith traditions.
- Helping congregations, seminaries and denominations to become sexually healthy faith communities.
- Educating the public and policymakers about a progressive religious vision of sexual morality, justice, and healing.

More than 5,400 clergy, professional religious educators and counselors, denominational and interfaith leaders, seminary presidents, deans and faculty members, representing more than 70 faith traditions, are endorsers in the Religious Institute's national network.

In 2010, the Religious Institute launched the Faithful Voices Network, a grassroots movement of people of faith from diverse traditions who support sexual health and justice in faith communities and society. The Faithful Voices Network advocates for increased commitment to sexual health, education and justice in congregations, denominations and communities. People of faith can join the Faithful Voices Network at religiousinstitute.org/faithfulvoices.

ABOUT THE AUTHOR

Debra W. Haffner is the Co-founder and President of the Religious Institute. An AASECT certified sexuality educator, she graduated from Union Theological Seminary and is an ordained Unitarian Universalist minister. She is the co-creator of the *Religious Declaration on Sexual Morality, Justice, and Healing.* She is the author of six books and many monographs for congregations on sexual health. In 2011, Widener University awarded her a Doctor of Public Service, h.c.

REFERENCES

1. J.B. Nelson, *Body Theology* (Louisville, Kentucky: Westminster/John Knox Press, 1992), p. 21.
2. S. Gibb, ed., *The Advocacy Manual for Sexual Health, Education, and Justice* (Boston: Unitarian Universalist Association and United Church of Christ Board for Homeland Ministries, 1999), p. 36.
3. The Pew Forum, *American Views on Religion, Politics, and Public Policy* (Washington, DC: The Pew Forum, April 2001).
4. The Surgeon General's Call To Action to Promote Sexual Health and Responsible Sexuality Behavior (Washington, DC: U.S. Public Health Service, July 2001).
5. Catechism of the Catholic Church, *Part Three: Life In Christ, Section Two: The Ten Commandments, Chapter Two: You Shall Love Your Neighbor As Yourself, Article 6: The Sixth Commandment, 1. "Male and Female He Created Them..."* www.vatican.va/archive/ENG0015/__P84.HTM, *accessed July 11, 2011.*
6. Church of the Brethren, Action of 1983 Annual Conference, *Human Sexuality from a Christian Perspective*, 1983, www.cobannualconference.org/ac_statements/83HumanSexuality.htm#I, accessed July 11, 2011.
7. Episcopal Church, Mind of the House Resolution adopted by the House of Bishops on March 18, 2003 meeting at Kanuga in North Carolina, *The Gift of Sexuality: A Theological Perspective*, www.episcopalchurch.org/documents/theologycomreport.pdf, accessed July 11, 2011.
8. Evangelical Lutheran Church in America, A Social Statement of the Evangelical Lutheran Church adopted August 19, 2009, *Human Sexuality: Gift and Trust*, www.elca.org/~/media/Files/Who%20We%20Are/Office%20of%20the%20Secretary/Assembly/CWA%202009%20Revised%20Social%20Statement%20HSGT%20FINAL.pdf, accessed July 11, 2011.
9. Federation of Reconstructionist Congregations and Havurot Reconstructionist Rabbinical Association, *Homosexuality and Judaism: The Reconstructionist Position—The Report of the Reconstructionist Commission on Homosexuality*, 1993, pp. 14–15.
10. Metropolitan Community Churches, *Statement of Purpose*, www.mcchurch.org/overview/, accessed July 12, 2011.
11. Central Conference of American Rabbis, *Reform Jewish Sexual Values*, 1998, www.rjyouthworker.urj.org/_kd/Items/actions.cfm?action=Show&item_id=1139&destination=ShowItem, accessed July 12, 2011.
12. M. Riley for the Unitarian Universalist Association, *Unitarian Universalist Perspectives: Religion, Morality and Sexuality*, 2011, www.uua.org/beliefs/uuperspectives/55657.shtml, accessed August 1, 2011.
13. The United Methodist Church, *Human Sexuality, The Book of Discipline of The United Methodist Church*, 2008, paragraph 161F, www.umc.org/site/apps/nlnet/content.aspx?c=lwL4KnN1Lt H&b=5066287&ct=6467529, accessed July 12, 2011.
14. United Church of Christ, E.A. Powers, ed., *Human Sexuality: Definitions and Actions, The Church—the Body*, 1977, www.ucc.org/education/polity/pdf-folder/human-sexuality-lth-98.pdf, accessed July 12, 2011.
15. L.B. Finer and S.K. Henshaw, "Disparities in rates of unintended pregnancy in the United States, 1994 and 2001," *Perspectives on Sexual and Reproductive Health*, 38(2): 90–96 (2006).
16. S. Alford and D. Hauser, *Adolescent Sexual Health in Europe and the United States: The Case For A Rights. Respect. Responsibility.® Approach,*

March 2011, Advocates for Youth 4th Edition, www.advocatesforyouth.org/publications/419?task=view, accessed August 1, 2011.

17. CDC, *Sexually Transmitted Diseases in the United States, 2008: National Surveillance Data for Chlamydia, Gonorrhea, and Syphilis* (Atlanta: U.S. Department of Health and Human Services, 2009), www.cdc.gov/std/stats08/trends.htm, accessed July 10, 2011.

18. Ibid.

19. Ibid.

20. CDC, *HIV in the United States* (July, 2010), www.cdc.gov/hiv/resources/factsheets/PDF/us.pdf, accessed July 10, 2011.

21. Ibid.

22. Ibid.

23. Gay, Lesbian, and Straight Education Network, *The 2009 National School Climate Survey* (2010), www.glsen.org/binary-data/GLSEN_ATTACHMENTS/file/000/001/1675-2.pdf, accessed July 11, 2011.

24. N. Ray, *Lesbian, Gay, Bisexual and Transgender Youth: An Epidemic of Homelessness* (2007), www.thetaskforce.org/downloads/HomelessYouth.pdf, accessed July 11, 2011.

25. J.D. Fortenberry, V. Schick, D. Herbenick, et al., "Sexual Behavior and Condom Use At Last Vaginal Intercourse: A National Sample of Adolescents Ages 14 to 17 Years," *Journal of Sexual Medicine*, 7 (Supplement s5) (2010): 305–314.

26. A.J. Sedlak, J. Mettenburg, M. Basena, I. Petta, K. McPherson, A. Greene, and S. Li, *Fourth National Incidence Study of Child Abuse and Neglect (NIS–4): Report to Congress*, (Washington, DC: U.S. Department of Health and Human Services, Administration for Children and Families, 2010), www.acf.hhs.gov/programs/opre/abuse_neglect/natl_incid/nis4_report_congress_full_pdf_jan2010.pdf, accessed July 11, 2011.

27. S.R. Dube, R.F. Anda, C.L. Whitfield, D.W. Brown, V.J. Felitti, M. Dong, W.H. Giles, "Long-term consequences of childhood sexual abuse by gender of victim," *American Journal Preventative Medicine*, June 28(5) (2005): 430–8.

28. U.S. Department of Justice, Bureau of Justice Statistics, *2007 National Crime Victimization Survey*, 2010, bjs.ojp.usdoj.gov/index.cfm?ty=pbdetail&iid=1743, accessed July 11, 2011.

29. P. Tjaden and N. Thoennes, *Prevalence, Incidence and Consequences of Violence Against Women: Findings from the National Violence Against Women Survey*, 1998, www.ncjrs.gov/pdffiles/172837.pdf, accessed July 11, 2011.

30. Department of Health and Human Services, Centers for Disease Control and Prevention, National Center for Injury Prevention and Control, *Costs of Intimate Partner Violence Against Women in the United States*, 2003, p. 14, www.cdc.gov/violenceprevention/pdf/IPVBook-a.pdf, accessed July 11, 2011.

31. Pan American Health Organization, *Promotion of Sexual Health: Recommendations for Action* (Washington, DC: PAHO, 2001), p. 6.

32. The Center for Sexuality and Religion, *The Role of Sexuality Education Within Seminaries, The Case for Comprehensive Sexuality Education Within the Context of Seminary Human and Theological Formation: A Report of the Ford Foundation*, 2002.

33. K.R. Meek, M.R. McMinn, T. Burnett, C. Mazzarella, and V. Voytenko, "Sexual Ethics Training in Seminary: Preparing Students to Manage Feelings of Sexual Attraction," *Pastoral Psychology*, 53(1) (2004): 63–79.

34. D.W. Haffner and T. Palmer, *Survey of Religious Progressives: A Report on Progressive Clergy Action and Advocacy for Sexual Justice*, 2009, www.religiousinstitute.org/sites/default/files/research_reports/surveyofreligiousprogressivespublicreportapril2009withcover.pdf, accessed July 12, 2011.

35. K.M. Ott, *Sex and the Seminary: Preparing Ministers for Sexual Health and Justice*, (Westport, CT: Religious Institute on Sexual Morality, Justice, and Healing and Union Theological Seminary in the City of New York, 2009).

36. Ibid.

37. J.S. Annon, *The Behavioral Treatment of Sexual Problems, Volume 1, Brief Therapy* (Honolulu, Hawaii: Mercantile Printing, 1974), pp. 100–105.

38. welfare.gov/systemwide/laws_policies/statutes/clergymandated.cfm

39. M. Lundquist Denton, L.D. Pearce and C. Smith, *Religion and Spirituality On the Path Through Adolescence, Research Report Number 8*, National Study of Youth and Religion (University of North Carolina at Chapel Hill, 2008).

40. Ibid.

41. Clapp, et al., *Faith Matters: Teenagers, Religion, and Sexuality* (Fort Wayne, IN: LifeQuest, 2010).

42. Centers for Disease Control, *Morbidity and Mortality Weekly Report*, June 4, 2010.

43. Regenerus et al., *Religion in the Lives of American Adolescents: A Review of the Literature: A Research Report of the National Study of Youth and Religion*, National Study of Youth and

Religion (University of North Carolina at Chapel Hill, 2003).

44. Clapp, et al., *Faith Matters: Teenagers, Religion, and Sexuality* (Fort Wayne, IN: LifeQuest, 2010).
45. Ibid.
46. Ibid.
47. Ibid.
48. Ibid.
49. Ibid.
50. Ibid.
51. National Campaign to Prevent Teen Pregnancy, *Faithful Nation* (Washington, DC: National Campaign, September 2001).
52. D. Haffner and K. Ott, *A Time to Speak, Third Edition* (Norwalk, CT: Religious Institute, 2011).
53. www.siecus.org/_data/global/ images/guidebooklines.pdf
54. E.O. Laumann, et al., *The Social Organization of Sexuality: Sexual Practices in the United States* (Chicago: University of Chicago Press, 1994), p. 88.

55 Ibid.
56. D. Haffner, *Beyond the Big Talk: Every Parent's Guidebook to Raising Sexually Healthy Teens* (New York: Newmarket Press, 2008).
57. P.B. Jung, M.E. Hunt, and R. Balakrishnan, *Good Sex: Feminist Perspectives from the World's Religions* (New Jersey: Rutgers University Press, 2001).
58. *The Book of Discipline of the United Methodist Church—2008*, (Nashville: The United Methodist Publishing House, 2008), P 304.3.
59 K.J. Terry, M.L. Smith, K. Schuth, J.R. Kelly, B. Vollman, and C. Massey, The Causes and Context of Sexual Abuse of Minors by Catholic Priests in the United States, 1950–2010: A Report Presented to the United States Conference of Catholic Bishops by the John Jay College Research Team, 2011, www.usccb.org/mr/ causes-and-context-of- sexual-abuse-of-minors-by-

catholic-priests-in-the-united- states-1950-2010.pdf, accessed August 2, 2011.
60. M. Chaves and D. Garland, "The Prevalence of Clergy Sexual Advances Toward Adults in Their Congregations," *Journal for the Scientific Study of Religion*, 48 (2009): 817–824.
61. D. Haffner, A *Time To Heal, Protecting Children & Ministering to Sex Offenders* (Fort Wayne, IN: LifeQuest, 2005).
62. The National Sex Offender Public Website, www.fbi.gov/ scams-safety/registry.
63. The Pew Forum, *Issue Ranks Lower on the Agenda: Support for Abortion Slips* (Washington, DC: The Pew Forum, October, 2009).
64. Catholics For Choice, "In Catholic Circles: The Church and Abortion," *Conscience: The News Journal of Catholic Opinion*, Autumn 2007.

38279559R00044

Made in the USA
San Bernardino, CA
02 September 2016